The Funniest People in Families: 250 Anecdotes

David Bruce

Published by David Bruce, 2022.

While every precaution has been taken in the preparation of this book, the publisher assumes no responsibility for errors or omissions, or for damages resulting from the use of the information contained herein.

THE FUNNIEST PEOPLE IN FAMILIES: 250 ANECDOTES

First edition. September 24, 2022.

Copyright © 2022 David Bruce.

ISBN: 979-8215282977

Written by David Bruce.

Table of Contents

Chapter 1: From Alcohol to Children 1

Chapter 2: From Christmas to Food 12

Chapter 3: From Gays and Lesbians to Husbands and Wives 25

Chapter 4: From Illness to Parents...35

Chapter 5: From Physicians to Work 46

Appendix A: Bibliography...58

Appendix B: About the Author 65

Appendix C: Some Books by David Bruce..66

Appendix C: Some Books by David Bruce..68

Cover Photograph for *The Funniest People in Families: 250 Anecdotes*:

Photographer: David Bruce

***

This is a short, quick, and easy read.

Anecdotes are usually short humorous stories. Sometimes they are thought-provoking or informative, not amusing.

Educate Yourself

Read Like A Wolf Eats

Be Excellent to Each Other

Books Then, Books Now, Books Forever

***

Do you know a language other than English? If you do, I give you permission to translate this book, copyright your translation, publish or self-publish it, and keep all the royalties for yourself. (Do give me credit, of course, for the original book.)

Chapter 1: From Alcohol to Children

Alcohol

• Comedian Jay Leno doesn't drink, smoke, or use illegal drugs. When Mavis Nicholson, who became his wife, asked for a drink early in their relationship, she almost did not become his wife. He told her, "Look, let me give you the money, and you can buy a blouse or something. I don't want to buy you a drink." With the $35 he gave her, she bought a blouse. (Mavis says, "I can't begin to tell you how absolutely *peculiar* I thought that was.")[1]

• Olivia Pound's father was a Nebraska judge in the 19th century. One day, an alcoholic lawyer attempted to argue a case before him, even though the lawyer was obviously inebriated. The judge listened for a few minutes, then banged his gavel and ruled, "This case is postponed for two weeks. The lawyer is trying to practice before two bars at the same time. It can't be done."[2]

Animals

• When Darci Kistler, a ballerina for the New York City Ballet, was growing up, her family had a pet alligator named Iggy. One day, Iggy got loose and made his way into the family swimming pool, where the family had a terrible time trying to catch him. Every time a family member tried to catch Iggy with a net, Iggy crushed the net in his jaws. Darci was relieved when Iggy was finally captured and returned to the pet store — she had noticed Iggy eying the family's dog and cat in a suspiciously hungry manner. Other family pets included snakes — once a boa constrictor was loose in the Kistler family house for a week.[3]

• On his TV show *House Party*, Art Linkletter interviewed a little girl whose fish had recently died. He asked whether the fish had gone to fish heaven, but the little girl replied, "No, I threw him down the toilet."[4]

Automobiles

• As a child, future Secretary of State Madeleine Albright traveled with her family as they moved to Denver, Colorado — a city that is known as the "Mile-High City" because it is one mile above sea level. Approaching the city, young Madeleine waited for the road to steeply climb one mile skyward, not realizing that the car had been gradually climbing higher for a long time.[5]

• Comedian Jay Leno really, really likes cars and motorcycles. In fact, his huge garage looks like a warehouse because it is so filled with his vehicular possessions. Still, whenever his mother visited him and wanted to borrow a car, he would tell her, "Mother, I'll *rent* you a car."[6]

Birth

• When Erma Bombeck's first book, *At Wit's End*, was published, she went on tour to publicize it. At one book signing, she spent three hours in a department store with a stack of her books on the desk at which she was sitting, but only two people approached her: A woman wanted directions to the ladies room, and a man asked her the price of the desk. Later, after she had written several best sellers, the lines of people waiting to have her autograph a book became very long. Once, a woman with an infant waited in line to have Ms. Bombeck sign a book. When Ms. Bombeck said that the infant was adorable, the woman replied, "Thank you. It was born in the line."[7]

• When comedian Henry Morgan was five years old, he was taken to a hospital where his mother was having a baby. He walked into her room, pointed to her stomach, and said, "I can see the baby." However, his mother smiled and said, "I've already had the baby." In his autobiography, *Here's Morgan!*, Mr. Morgan writes, "This gift of saying the right thing at the right time has been with me all my life."[8]

• Entertainer Art Linkletter's daughter Sharon was giving birth. Because her physician knew her only by her married name, he was shocked when Mr. Linkletter showed up at the hospital. He told Sharon, "Guess who's waiting to see you on the other side of those doors — Art Linkletter!" Sharon shocked him further by saying, "Why shouldn't he be here? He's my father."[9]

• The most comedian Eddie Cantor ever laughed was in response to a line by Amanda, his four-year-old granddaughter. Mr. Cantor was in the hospital for minor surgery, and Amanda was allowed to see him as long as she was a good girl. At the end of the visit, Amanda asked, "Wasn't I a good girl, Grandpa?" Then she added, "So now may I see the baby?"[10]

• While Eve Arden, famous especially for her radio and TV lead character in *Our Miss Brooks*, was having labor pains for her son (Douglas), she ran into one small problem — nurses in the pre-labor room kept asking her for her autograph.[11]

Birthdays

• Carmine Buete was a 10-year-old boy with AIDS who lived near New York City. He caught AIDS from his mother, who died when he was a year and three months old — he was so young when his mother died that he couldn't remember her. Still, whenever the wind blew open the door of his home, he would say that it was his mother. On his mother's birthday, he used to send her a helium-filled balloon by standing on a porch, releasing the balloon, and letting it soar into the sky. After Carmine died on July 13, 1996, his family started sending balloons to him on his birthday.[12]

• Comedian and announcer Henry Morgan is married to an intelligent woman. On one of his birthdays, an old friend of Henry's called him on the telephone to talk over old times. Throughout the rest of the day at half-hour intervals, more old friends of Henry's kept calling him. He found out later that his wife, Karen, had spent a week tracking down his old friends and assigning them a time to call.[13]

• Humorist Frank Sullivan enjoyed birthdays very much, but he enjoyed even more making jokes at his friends' expense. A friend who sent him a congratulatory telegram sometimes received a telegram like this in reply: "Your telegram on my birthday today will suffice until you can find time to send me some more substantial gift. Thanking you in advance, Mr. Sullivan."[14]

Books

• An 8th-grade student didn't read a book for her book report, but instead made up a book and completely invented the plot and characters while telling her teacher that she had bought the book at a bookstore and had left it at home and therefore couldn't remember such things as its publisher and copyright. The student received a good grade on the book report, but the teacher wrote a note on her report, asking where he could buy a copy of the book as a present for his niece. The student was so unnerved by the teacher's note that she never cheated again.[15]

• Reading can educate people. Author Walter Dean Myers once received a letter from a teenager who had been watching television coverage of the Persian Gulf War and was so excited that he could hardly wait to turn 17 so he could join the Army and fight in a war. However, after reading Mr. Myers' *Fallen Angels*, a realistic war book, he decided that he did not want to fight after all. *Fallen Angels* was a tribute to Mr. Myers' younger brother, Sonny, who died two days after being sent to Vietnam.[16]

• Author Judy Blume loved books even when she was a little girl. In fact, she loved the picture book *Madeline* so much that after borrowing it from a library, she didn't want to return it. Instead, she hid the book and then told her mother that she had lost it.[17]

Brothers

• Two brothers, one of whom was married and the other single, farmed the same land together, and they split the harvest equally. The brother who was single felt that the brother who was married should have more of the harvest, so he would secretly take sacks of grain from his storehouse and put them in the married brother's storehouse. However, the brother who was married worried that the brother who was single was lonely, and in order to allow his brother to buy nice things for himself, he would secretly take sacks of grain from his storehouse and put them in the single brother's storehouse. Year after year, both brothers received an equal number of sacks of grain, and neither understood why.[18]

• When he was growing up, Cordell Brown and Phil, his brother, played their own version of dodge ball — instead of throwing a ball, Phil threw very ripe peaches at Cordell. Because Cordell had cerebral palsy, he seldom got out of the way of the peaches, so he became a mess very quickly. Today, they laugh when they recall those games. (Cordell is a wonderful man who has founded a summer camp called Camp Echoing Hills and several residential homes for handicapped adults in Ohio.)[19]

• At a trial, the prosecutor tried to get Wilson Mizner to admit that he was covering up in order to save his brother, Addison. The prosecutor asked Wilson, who was on the witness stand, "You love your brother, don't you? You have a great affection for him, don't you?" Unfortunately for the prosecutor, Wilson had lots of experience on the witness stand. He replied, "I have a vague regard for him."[20]

Chanukah

• On Chanukah, parents customarily give gifts, such as coins, to their children. One Chanukah, actor Elliott Gould told his children, "Tonight, instead of money, I'm going to give you total honesty and truth, which is more important." Molly, his daughter, replied, "But you give us that every night."[21]

Children

• Maud Gruss was born into a French circus family, and at age three, she decided to make an unscheduled public appearance in a balancing act. A cousin named Eddy Ringenbach was performing with his sister (Isabelle), and with Maud's brother (Armand). Eddy was lying on his back, using his legs to support a ladder, on which Isabelle and Armand were performing tricks. Suddenly, young Maud walked out, dressed in a pink tutu, climbed over Eddy, and started to climb up the ladder. The circus audience started to applaud, and Maud, hearing the applause, let go of the ladder and started to applaud, too. As she applauded, she began to fall. Isabelle and Armand immediately jumped off the ladder. Isabelle did a back flip, and Armand did a front flip. When Armand landed, he was holding Maud safely in his arms. The circus audience thought they had witnessed a perfectly performed, much-rehearsed trick, and they gave three-year-old Maud and the other performers an enormous ovation.[22]

• When world-class women's gymnastics coaches Bela and Marta Karolyi defected from Romania to the United States, they did not know English and had a difficult time learning it. When they brought their young daughter (Andrea) to the United States, she also did not know English, and they were worried about her. They tried a public school and a private school, but at both schools the teachers did not pay particular attention to Andrea, who sat silently. Eventually, however, Andrea picked up English on her own. Bela saw her speaking to some American kids, and he asked if she was speaking Romanian or Hungarian to them. Andrea replied, "I'm talking like everybody else." After that experience, Bela and Marta decided that "the best teachers were the children."[23]

• Operatic tenor Leo Slezak knew how to get the truth from his children when they were small — all he had to do was to tell them that he would ask the Angel what had happened and the Angel would tell him. One day, his young son, Walter, refused to eat his supper. He put the food in his mouth, but he would not swallow it. He then left the room for a moment, returned, and said with a big grin, "I've eaten it now!" Mr. Slezak was doubtful, so he said that he would ask the Angel. Feeling cocky, Walter told him to go ahead and do just that. Mr. Slezak then said that the Angel had told him that Walter had given his food to the family dog, and Walter turned pale and stammered, "How could the Angel find that out?"[24]

• While the Three Stooges were performing live on stage, Sandy, the five-year-old niece of Larry Fine — the balding but not bald Stooge — was in the audience, watching as the Stooges slapped each other and poked each other's eyes. However, at one point, when Moe led a screaming Larry around the stage after sticking his finger up Larry's nose, Sandy started yelling, "You're hurting my Uncle Larry! You're hurting my Uncle Larry!" Larry immediately came over to her and explained that he was only pretending to be hurt, then he rejoined the act to the loud applause of the audience. As for Moe, he was laughing so hard that it took a while for the act to continue.[25]

• Horror writer Anne Rice got her first name from an unusual source: herself. Her name at birth was Howard Allen O'Brien. This name is unusual in itself, and she was given it in part because her father, Howard, had been bullied at school because some other children thought "Howard" sounded like a girl's name. On the first day young Howard started attending Redemptorist School in New Orleans, a nun asked her for her name. Young Howard replied, "It's Anne!" This name turned out to be OK with her mother, who said, "If she wants to be Anne, it's Anne." Anne received the rest of her adult name after she married Stan Rice.[26]

• Early in her gymnastics career, when she was still a pre-teen, Shannon Miller attended a meet in Las Vegas, and she stayed at the Circus Circus Hotel. When she returned home, she had a lot of stuffed animals with her. Her mother asked where she had gotten them, and young Shannon joked, "Gambling." The real story was that a man in the hotel had asked if she liked stuffed animals. She had replied, "Sure," and he had given her a bunch of stuffed animals he had just won. (Her parents did talk to her about not accepting gifts from strangers.)[27]

• While making a personal appearance in Chicago, TV's Mister Rogers asked if anyone in the audience had anything they wanted to share. A small boy spoke up: "Mister Rogers, I just wear diapers at night now." Of course, the audience wondered how Mister Rogers would react to this sharing. He replied to the boy, "Well, that's very important, and it's up to you when you'll give up your diapers at night. I'm really proud of the ways you're growing." This made the small boy very happy and the audience breathed a sigh of relief at Mister Rogers' answer.[28]

• Frank Bunker Gilbreth raised a dozen children in the early 20th century. With such a large brood, he wasn't above getting a break on expenses now and then. Whenever he came to a toll road, he would look at the toll keeper, identify his nationality, then say, using the appropriate accent, "Do my Irishmen [or Dutchmen, or Scotsmen] come cheaper by the dozen?" Often, the reply would come back, "Irishmen, is it? And I might have known it. ... The Lord Jesus didn't mean for any family like that to pay toll on my road. Drive through on the house."[29]

• As a child athlete, Robin Campbell competed in many national and international track and field events, necessitating absences from home. During one long absence, she rejoiced that she had gotten out of doing the dishes, which she did each Monday when she was home. However, her family believed that children should do chores, so when Robin returned home, she discovered that she had been scheduled to wash dishes for a whole week so she could catch up to the work done by her siblings while she was away.[30]

• Chase, the young son of Christian writer Dale Hanson Bourke, had a babysitter who had lost a leg when she was a young girl in Peru, leaving her with a wooden leg that caused her to limp. One day, Ms. Bourke saw the babysitter and young Chase walking together, and she noticed that her son was limping before he came running to her. The babysitter, Doris, explained, "He always walks that way with me." When Ms. Bourke asked why, Doris replied, "So we can be alike."[31]

• While on his own as a youngster after running away from home, comedian W.C. Fields would sometimes crawl through a punched-out window into a cellar where he would sleep by a furnace. This was very good quarters for him at that time. Unfortunately, one day he discovered that the window had been fixed, probably because he had been stealing the housewife's preserves. "The thing taught me a lesson," he said later. "You've got to know where to stop."[32]

• When he was a 12-year-old boy living in New Concord, Ohio, astronaut John Glenn wanted to be a Boy Scout, but there was no local troop for him to join. No problem. He and his friends organized their own scouting group and called it the Ohio Rangers. They engaged in such activities as swimming upstream, hiking in snow, and sleeping outdoors in the rain. Mr. Glenn says, "We told one another we were tougher than Scouts — so tough they wouldn't have us."[33]

• Lady Astor, the first woman to sit in either of the British Houses of Parliament, was once heckled by a woman who shouted, "My children are as good as yours." Lady Astor replied, "As which of mine? I've got some worse than any of yours — but I might have one who is better." Another time, a man shouted, "Your husband's a millionaire, ain't he?" Lady Astor replied, "I should certainly hope so — that's why I married him."[34]

• The two young sons of Francis Hodgson Burnett, author of *A Little Princess* and *The Secret Garden*, supported James Garfield during his Presidential election. The boys used to hang from one of their upstairs windows and shout, "Rah for Garfield!" After he was elected, they were invited to the White House, where they rode their bicycles in the halls and knocked down Senators and other VIPs.[35]

• When R' Dov Ber of Mezritch was an eight-year-old boy, the home of his family burned down. His mother began to cry, and so he asked why she was crying. She replied that it wasn't because of the house, but because the fire had destroyed a document recording the family tree, which went back to R' Yochanan HaSandlar. The child replied, "Don't worry, mother. I will be the start of a new family tree."[36]

• Groucho Marx' young daughter, Melinda, came to him one night and asked him to tell her the bedtime story "Little Red Riding Hood."

Because Groucho was busy, he asked her if someone else could tell the story to her. But Melinda insisted that he told the story better than anyone else. When Groucho asked why, she explained, "Because you put more food in Red Riding Hood's basket."[37]

• Children loved comedian Joe E. Brown. He tells about a letter written by one of the mothers of those children. Just six years old, the child saw one of Mr. Brown's movies, then asked his mother, "Mommy, when Joe E. Brown dies, will he go to Heaven?" The child's mother replied, "Why, of course, darling." "Golly, Mommy," the child said. "Won't God laugh!"[38]

• A friend of author Sharon Salzberg had a four-year-old son whose caregiver, to whom he was very attached, was going to move away to live with her sister and so would not be able to take care of him anymore. She explained this carefully to him, and he said, "Mommy, tell me that story again but with a different ending."[39]

• On the First Sunday in Lent, the pastor visited a Sunday School class taught by Rolf E. Aaseng. The pastor wore his clerical vestments and spoke about why the vestments' colors change during the year. One little girl was very impressed and later told her mother, "God came to Sunday School today!"[40]

• A church-going young mother and her two young daughters were shopping in a health-food store when a tall, strong, white-robe-wearing elderly man with long, white hair and beard walked in. The younger daughter stared at the man until her older sister told her, "No, Regan, it's not God."[41]

• The Reverend James Bence was visiting the family of the Reverend Ed Crandall when he asked Crandall's young son, "Well, Steve, have you been a good boy lately?" Steve answered, "Yes." The Reverend Bence then asked, "Are you good all of the time?" Young Steve answered, "Well, are *you*?"[42]

• A prosthesis (an artificial limb) is a useful thing, but it can cause some strange phone calls. A mother once received this call from a camp for children with cancer: "Mrs. Anderson? Robin broke a leg on the trail. Could you please send up another one on a plane?"[43]

• English entertainer Joyce Grenfell had an Uncle Buck who was a rolling stone. According to family lore, when his youngest child was being taught the prayer, "Our father which art in Heaven," the child looked up and said, "Mama, where's Papa gone now?"[44]

• Art Linkletter used to interview very young children, and he had great success asking them what their parents had told them not to say on the show. A little girl once responded, "She told me not to announce that she was pregnant."[45]

• As a child, violinist Mischa Elman played Beethoven's *Kreutzer Sonata*, which includes some long pauses, before some relatives. During one of the pauses, his aunt asked, "Why don't you play something you know, Mischa?"[46]

• As a child, Frida Kahlo was mischievous. Sometimes, she soaped the steps near where Mexican artist Diego Rivera was working, in the hope that he would slip on the stairs and fall. When she grew up, she married Mr. Rivera.[47]

• Country comedian Jerry Clower has children who can make him laugh. When Katy Burns, his daughter, was four, she pulled off her gloves, then called, "Daddy! Daddy! If I had one more finger, I could count to 11."[48]

• Ballerina Anna Pavlova was made very happy when she received a copy of a child's essay that began, "Once I saw a fairy. Her name was Anna Pavlova."[49]

Chapter 2: From Christmas to Food

Christmas

• Early in the 20th century, a custom in some parts of the United States was to tie presents to a Christmas tree at the church and have Santa Claus come to the church for a party and pass out all the presents. At one such Christmas Eve party, a little girl, the daughter of the richest and most miserly man in town, showed up for the party and the passing out of presents. (Her older brothers stayed away because they realized that their father was too stingy to put a present on the tree for them.) As the evening passed, the little girl's name wasn't called even once. Fortunately, Alyene Porter, the youngest daughter of the preacher, noticed what was happening. She told her mother, who re-wrapped Alyene's present to her, a bottle of perfume, and put the little girl's name on it, then surreptitiously hung it on the tree. When Santa Claus finally called her name, the little girl cried out, "He did call it! He did call it! I did get a present!"[50]

• Christmases when religious writer Dale Hanson Bourke was a little girl were sometimes surprising. One Christmas the presents were placed in the shower stall. Her father explained that since their house didn't have a fireplace, Santa Claus must have squeezed through the water pipes to come inside and leave presents. On one Christmas Eve, little Dale was allowed to choose one present to open, so she chose the biggest present. However, her parents had guessed that she would choose that present so they had filled it with nuts. Although everyone laughed, her parents knew that she was disappointed, so they let her open the rest of her presents.[51]

• One Christmas, Pope John XXIII went to a children's hospital to visit the patients. One child, Silvio Colagrande, had been blind, but could now see because a dying priest, Don Gnocchi, had willed his eyes to Silvio and the corneas had been transplanted. Upon seeing the

Pope, Silvio called out, "I see you with Don Gnocchi's eyes." Another child, seven-year-old Carmine Gemma, had recently become blind as the result of an attack of meningitis. He told Pope John XXIII, "You're the Pope, I know, but I can't see you." The Pope held Carmine's hands for a while, then he murmured, "We are all blind, sometimes."[52]

• When poet Nikki Giovanni was a small child, her parents, Gus and Yolande, didn't always have the money necessary to buy what their two young daughters wanted. One Christmas, their two daughters wanted bicycles, but Mr. and Mrs. Giovanni could afford to buy them only roller skates. However, they did figure out a way to make them happier about not getting bicycles although other children in the neighborhood had. They told her, "Isn't it terrible that their parents gave them bicycles when it's so cold? They won't be able to ride until spring."[53]

• When Leo Slezak's son (Walter) was eight years old, he wrote out a list of presents for Santa Claus to bring to him. However, the governess mentioned to Mr. Slezak that Walter didn't believe in Santa Claus any more. When Mr. Slezak asked Walter why he had written out a list of presents for Santa Claus, little Walter replied, "I didn't want to spoil the pleasure for you and Mommy."[54]

• On Christmas, Pope John XXIII (who was named Angelo Giuseppe Roncalli at his birth) sometimes visited children in a hospital. He once asked a boy what his name was. The boy replied, "Giuseppe." Not knowing who his visitor was, the boy asked, "What's your name?" The Pope answered, "Oh, my name is Giuseppe, too, but now everybody calls me John."[55]

Couples

• In the old days, William Boake wished to court Euphemia Birkett, but her guardian, Catherine Tew, disliked him. One day, Mr. Boake arrived to visit Ms. Birkett, but Ms. Tew made sure that her charge was upstairs and out of sight. Mr. Boake was not to be trifled with, so he ran upstairs, and Ms. Tew tried to stop him by grabbing one of the tails of his coat, only to have the tail tear off in her hand. After he and Ms. Birkett were married, Mr. Boake kept the one-tailed coat as a souvenir of his courtship.[56]

• When Jack Gilford was courting Madeline Lee, he was working at a resort and called her long distance. The telephone operator at the resort listened to all their conversations and found them very entertaining. Once, after a conversation more than usually filled with passion and drama, Mr. Gilford asked the telephone operator, "How much do I owe you?" With a sob in her throat, the telephone operator said, "Never mind. There's no charge tonight."[57]

• A missionary couple stayed at the home of an elderly widow. When they went to bed, they discovered that the bedding was very wrinkled and very dirty, but they slept in the bed anyway. The next morning, the widow explained, "For years there have been so many holy people who have slept in that bed that I've never been able to [bring myself to] change it."[58]

• Track superstar Mary Decker frequently wrote an early boyfriend when she was away from him. While in New York, she wrote him four letters in two days and then telephoned him on the third day — she hadn't received a letter from him yet, and she was worried that something had happened to him.[59]

• A friend of lesbian comedian Judy Carter wore a wedding ring to work. When her co-workers asked what her husband did, she replied, "*She* works for a pharmacy."[60]

Daughters

• Rabbi Joseph Telushkin once watched his two daughters playing together nicely, and he commented to a friend named Dennis Prager how much pleasure this sight was giving him. Mr. Prager asked, "Doesn't it give you more pleasure than if one of your daughters said 'I love you, Daddy' but didn't act nicely to her sister?" Rabbi Telushkin answered, "Of course." Mr. Prager then said, "I imagine God is the same way. He derives greater pleasure when people are good to each other than when they are 'good' to Him but not to each other."[61]

• When Robin, Bob Dole's daughter, was young, she was a great fan of a British rock band, so Senator Dole wrote the British embassy to find out if the band could play at his daughter's high school as a surprise. Unfortunately, he received a reply saying that the Beatles would be too busy to oblige during their first American tour.[62]

• Comic actor Robert Morley once embarrassed his daughter by attempting to surf in Hawaii — he was unable even to mount the surfboard. When his mortified daughter told him, "People were laughing at you," he was unperturbed and replied, "Usually they have to pay to laugh at me."[63]

Death

• Ann Weeks of Lexington, Kentucky, suffered the loss of her husband. Unfortunately, for weeks following the funeral, people kept telephoning and asking for her husband because they were unaware that he had died. One day, a salesman called and asked for him. Ms. Weeks replied, "I'm sorry, Paul is deceased. I'm his wife. May I help you?" The salesman didn't say anything about her husband's death, but he did tell Ms. Weeks that he was with the Appliance Warranty Center and was calling to remind her that a warranty on an appliance had run out and she needed to renew it. Ms. Weeks replied that she had decided not to renew that warranty. The salesman, annoyed, said, "Well, I'm sure your dead husband would want you to renew." Not liking to be manipulated, Ms. Weeks replied, "Funny you should mention it, but just hours before Paul died he said, 'Honey, whatever you do, don't renew the appliance warranty!'" The salesman hung up.[64]

• Near the end of his life, Al Capp, creator of *Li'l Abner*, was confined to a wheelchair. One day he asked his wife if she had any silver candlesticks and plain white candles in the house. She did, so he asked, "Would you light those candles and put them on the mantelpiece. Tonight, I mean. This is Friday, isn't it, Catherine?" It was Friday, and

Catherine did as her husband requested. Later, Elliott Caplin, Al's brother, explained the significance of the candles. In their family, the person who most revered the Sabbath and lit the candles and said the prayers had been their mother. As Al Capp sat in his apartment, knowing that he was dying, he was thinking about his mother.[65]

• Comedian Beatrice Lillie once visited her mother's grave and saw that a small, freshly dug grave was nearby. Filled with pity at the death of an infant, she spent a few weeks tending the grave and planting flowers — originally intended for her own mother's grave — all around it. Later, a friend asked her if she was still tending the grave. She replied that she had discovered that it was the grave of an 85-year-old man, so "I dug up every god*mn plant and put them back on my mother's grave."[66]

• Philosopher Richard Watson's father knew that he was dying of cancer. He told his son, "I'm dying. Don't give me any of that crap I'm not." His son replied, "OK, so you're dying. Now what?" In reply, he just grinned. Just before he died, one of his favorite nieces and her husband visited him. At the end of their visit, the husband said, "I want you to be sitting up in a chair next time I see you." He replied, "You don't see too many people buried sitting up."[67]

• A man once drew up a will in which he left everything to his wife and three sons. He then asked the Chafetz Chaim to look over the will and criticize it. After looking over the will, the Chafetz Chaim pointed out that the man had overlooked an important beneficiary: his soul. The will made no provision for charity, and the man's soul deserved to be considered in the will.[68]

• At a funeral, brightly colored clothing is regarded as inappropriate, but not even family members are required to wear black, although many do. Etiquette expert Grace Fox knows a woman who wore a lovely blue dress at the funeral of her husband and touchingly explained that it was her husband's favorite dress.[69]

• After her grandmother died, track superstar Mary Decker ran a race on an indoor track in Los Angeles, California. She cried the entire distance and finished last.[70]

• In his will, comedian Jack Benny made the provision that his wife, Mary Livingstone, be given a perfect red rose every day for the rest of her life.[71]

Easter

• As a teenager, Connie, the daughter of the Rev. Frederick L. Haynes, liked sunrise Easter services even more than Christmas. Now a mother with three sons, each Easter she drags her sons out of bed before sunrise to get ready for the sunrise service. Sometimes they ask her, "Why, Mom?" She replies, "We are Easter people."[72]

Education

• When Ralph Bunche was very young, his mother told him, "My boy, don't ever let anything take away your hope and faith and dreams." After his mother died, Ralph attended high school, but despite high grades, he was kept out of the city-wide honor society known as the Ephebian Society simply because he was black. He thought about quitting school, but then he remembered what his mother had told him and so he stayed in school. In 1922, he became valedictorian of his high school. In 1934, he earned a Ph.D. in political science and international relations from Harvard University. In 1950, because of his work with the United Nations, he became the first African American to win the Nobel Peace Prize.[73]

• World-class women's gymnastics coach Bela Karolyi was born in Romania and so after he defected to the United States he did not know English well. One day, Andrea, his daughter, came home from school and requested help with an assignment: to make a New Year's resolution. Bela was outraged, screaming, "No revolution, no revolution in my house. Absolutely no revolution." His wife, Marta, came home later and asked why Bela wasn't helping their daughter. Bela replied, "Marta, her teacher wants us to help her start a revolution. I won't be a part of that!" Fortunately, his wife was able to explain the homework assignment to him.[74]

• When Angelo Giuseppe Roncalli (who was later to be Pope John XXIII) was a child, he became lazy in his studies, so his parents gave him a letter and sent him to give it to a local priest. Angelo was suspicious about the letter's contents, so he opened it and read it. After reading that the letter told the priest to give him a good scolding for not studying harder, Angelo tore up the letter and threw it away. (Despite not being scolded by the priest, Angelo did thereafter pay more attention to his studies.)[75]

• A young man, the son of a preacher, attended a Bible college. Coming home for the weekend, he decided to do his Bible study homework while sitting in church as his father preached. Later, his father asked what he had been doing. The young man confessed that he had been doing his homework, and his father asked, "Don't you think you should be listening to the sermon?" Today, the young man says that he is the only person ever to get in trouble for studying the Bible in church.[76]

• One day, an elderly couple met the president of Harvard. They told him that they would like to know more about Harvard before making a contribution in memory of their son, who had been killed in war. However, the elderly couple was plainly dressed and the president of Harvard quickly brushed them off. So the elderly couple went to northern California and used their money to establish Stanford University, in memory of Leland Stanford, their son.[77]

• In 1958, Suzanne Farrell — at that time she was a very young Cincinnati, Ohio, dance student whose real name was Roberta Ficker — learned that the famous New York City Ballet was performing in Bloomington, Indiana. Her mother supported her daughter's dance ambitions, and so she wrote a note to excuse her daughter's absence (because of illness, she wrote) and they took a day off to enjoy the dance performance.[78]

• A little girl went to kindergarten for the first time with her mother walking her the short distance to school. After her mother had left, the little girl needed to go to the bathroom, so her teacher said she could leave the classroom. The little girl then walked home, where she went to the bathroom. Later, the little girl was surprised to learn that there were bathrooms at school, just like there were at home.[79]

• A cat walked into an elementary school classroom, where the young students immediately gathered around it, fed it milk, and tried to guess its sex. A little girl said, "I know how we can tell its sex." Her teacher wasn't especially thrilled to hear this, and she was relieved when the little girl continued, "We can vote on it."[80]

• English schoolboys sometimes make a lot of noise when applauding, including stomping with their feet. Whenever his schoolboys stomped, Frederick Andrews, the headmaster of Ackworth, would tell them, "I like you to applaud with all your hearts, but not with all your soles."[81]

Fathers
• As a teenager, President Bill Clinton's Secretary of State Madeleine Albright went on dates that were not like the typical dates of today's American girls. Although she had moved to the United States as a girl, Ms. Albright was born in Czechoslovakia, and her father followed old-world ideas about dating. He would let Ms. Albright's boyfriend drive her to wherever the date would happen, but he followed them in his own car and went on the date with them. After the date was over, he drove his daughter home while her boyfriend followed them in his car, then Mr. Albright invited his daughter's boyfriend in for milk and cookies. Needless to say, Ms. Albright didn't keep boyfriends for long. (Nevertheless, she did get married and gave birth to three daughters.)[82]

• Comedian Albert Brooks' father was funny. In a restaurant, he would sometimes stand up and announce to the other diners, "I want your attention, all of you. This boy [Albert] is not eating his vegetables."

As a high school student, Albert did an imitation of escape artist Harry Houdini as an incompetent who couldn't even get his hands out of his own pockets. This impressed family friend Carl Reiner so much that when Johnny Carson asked him on *The Tonight Show* who were the funniest people he knew, he named Mel Brooks and young Albert.[83]

• Choreographer Martha Graham's father was a doctor. When she was a child, he showed her a drop of water on a slide and asked what she saw. Of course, she replied that she saw a drop of water. He asked if the water was pure, and she answered that it was. Dr. Graham then asked her to look at it with a microscope. She did, and she saw lots of bacteria in the water. "Yes, it is impure," Dr. Graham said. "Just remember this all your life, Martha. You must look for the truth."[84]

• Just before the short program at the 2001 World Championships, figure skater Michelle Kwan had a problem when the heel of one skate came loose. According to figure skating rules, if you don't have your equipment prepared to skate when your name is called, you are disqualified. Fortunately, Ms. Kwan's father came to the rescue. He fixed the heel by using six screws — and three tubes of super glue. (Yes, Michelle won the gold medal.)[85]

• Kerry Strug's father once told her that she was his least expensive child, because the only gifts she ever wanted were leotards and because she never wore out her shoes since she was always walking on her hands. (Later, Ms. Strug became an elite gymnast and her father had to pay out big bucks for her training — the training paid off with a gold medal at the 1996 Olympics in Atlanta.)[86]

• Olympic gymnast Shannon Miller once performed a very bad vault that sent her crashing to the mat. Her father, Ron, is a university professor who uses video of that vault to teach his class some principles of physics. The agreement Shannon and her father made is that after he shows the video of the very bad vault, he has to show a video of her performing the vault flawlessly.[87]

• Cordell Brown has cerebral palsy and two sons. (He also founded a summer camp called Camp Echoing Hills and several residential homes for handicapped adults in Ohio.) He never asked his sons about his disability until they were grown, then he asked if having a father with cerebral palsy had made life difficult for them. They answered, "Dad, you've just always been Dad."[88]

• Gay comedian Bob Smith warned his boyfriend, Tom, that his father, a retired state trooper, judged people by their handshake, so that when they met Tom would know to give him a firm handshake. Bob's father once told him, "Bob, I like all your friends because all the men have very solid handshakes, and come to think of it, all the women do, too."[89]

• A Jewish man heard that his father was ill; however, visiting his father would involve an expensive train journey. Knowing that Jewish law does not require a child to spend money to honor a parent, he asked Rabbi Hayyim of Brisk to make a ruling. Rabbi Hayyim quickly made the ruling: "You are not required to spend the money — walk!"[90]

• Joe Garagiola led a very busy life in broadcasting for a long time. How busy was he? He walked into the door of his house one day, and his wife told their three-year-old daughter, "It's Daddy!" His daughter asked, "What channel?" Mr. Garagiola says, "When your own kids only recognize you when you're on TV, it's time to do some thinking."[91]

• Meredith Willson's father, whose favorite movie actress was Anita Stewart, was as stubborn as only a person from Iowa can be. Mr. Willson's father referred to her as "An-eye-ta," and when Mr. Willson told him that she called herself "An-ee-ta," he replied, "She's mistaken."[92]

• A good father had a bad son who gave him trouble and heartbreak. The son even abandoned God. When the father complained to the founder of Hasidism, the Baal Shem Tov, and asked what he should do, the Baal Shem Tov replied, "Love him more than ever."[93]

• A contestant on the old TV show *Name That Tune* was trying to guess a song that was titled "Christopher Columbus." The host of the show gave her a hint: "If he didn't do what he did, you wouldn't be here today." The contestant answered, "My father."[94]

• Comedian Sam Kinison's father was a preacher. Whenever word of Sam's often wild and crazy lifestyle came back home, his father would tell his congregation, "I've been praying for your children for years. Now it's time for you to pray for one of mine."[95]

Food

• This is a story told by Irving Cramer, the Executive Director of MAZON: A Jewish Response to Hunger. A kindergarten teacher once asked her students how many of them had eaten breakfast that morning. About half had, so the teacher asked those who hadn't eaten, why not. Some didn't eat breakfast because they didn't like what was served or because they had gotten up late, but one child said, "It wasn't my turn." The teacher asked the child to explain, and he said, "There are five kids in my family. But we don't have enough money to buy enough food so that everybody can eat breakfast every day. We take turns eating breakfast, and today, it wasn't my turn."[96]

• In 1994, ice dancers Irina Lobacheva and Ilia Averbukh competed at the World Championships, finishing a respectable 13th. However, the next year this married couple had trouble finding enough food to eat and enough training time in their native Russia and so finished 15th at the 1995 World Championships. Therefore, they moved to Delaware in the United States where they found plenty of food and training time, enabling them to finish 6th at the 1996 World Championships. They kept improving and finally got on the medals stand by finishing 3rd at the 2001 World Championships.[97]

• When Aung San Suu Kyi was a little girl in Burma, she was afraid of the dark, but she wanted to overcome her fear. Each evening, her mother made hot milk for each of the children to drink, but Suu Kyi didn't like her milk hot, so she would leave it to cool, and later each evening, she would drink the milk alone in the dark. She says, "The first few days my heart would go 'thump, thump, thump,' but after five or six days I got quite used to it." In 1991, she won the Nobel Peace Prize for her efforts to bring freedom to the people of Burma.[98]

• Actor Walter Matthau's mother didn't know to cook. One of the things she didn't know how to cook was meat loaf — which she steamed along with assorted vegetables. One day, Mr. Matthau and Jennie, his nine-year-old daughter, went to her house for dinner. After dinner, Mr. Matthau noticed that Jennie's back pocket had a large wet spot, and he asked her about it. She answered, "Don't tell grandma. Please, don't tell grandma." She had stuffed the meatloaf and steamed vegetables in her back pocket.[99]

• A large family — with seven children between age three to age 13 — walked into a restaurant. Because so many young children were in the family, the waitresses and management were worried that they would be rowdy and disturb the other patrons of the restaurant. However, the children knew their manners and behaved correctly — no yelling, no fighting, no playing. When the family had finished eating, the waitress presented them with their bill — with 10 percent deducted for good behavior![100]

• Comedian Eddie Cantor's daughter, Marilyn, grew up to become a good cook — and a good wit. Once she had several people over for dinner; as she was carrying the entree to the table, she dropped it, and suddenly the floor was awash with shrimps swimming in chili sauce. The guests fell silent, but Marilyn said, "Don't just stand there — dig in!"[101]

• Rolf E. Aaseng was once asked by his wife to make some biscuits. He looked in the open cookbook, found that the recipe was for 48 biscuits, so he made 48 biscuits out of the dough. However, his wife had forgotten to tell him that when she made biscuits she halved the recipe. Fortunately, the family dog enjoyed the extra biscuits.[102]

• As pioneers traveled from east to west across North America in covered wagons, often they had very little change in their diets. One pioneer woman with a sense of humor wrote that about the only change in the diet of her and her family consisted of eating bacon and bread instead of bread and bacon.[103]

• Lydia Parker White, a Quaker, was known for her homemade cookies, and her grandchildren frequently asked her for cookies, something that sometimes upset their parents. Once, her granddaughter visited her and after greeting her, said, "Mama told me not to ask thee for cookies today."[104]

Chapter 3: From Gays and Lesbians to Husbands and Wives

Gays and Lesbians

• When financial writer Andrew Tobias finally came out to his parents, he called his mother on the telephone and told her — many of his gay friends regard this way of coming out as lacking grace. Her first words to him were, "Don't tell your father — promise me." After nearly two years, she gave her son permission to tell his father. When he did come out to his father — who wasn't surprised — he also gave him an autobiography about being gay that he had published under a pseudonym. His father stayed up all night and read *The Best Little Boy in the World* twice, and he cried because he hadn't realized that his son was a homosexual and was going through so much pain and so he hadn't been there for Andrew. Both parents accepted their son's homosexuality. At a Thanksgiving dinner, his father met Andrew's significant other, Charles Nolan, and told Andrew that Charles "seems like a very fine young man." His mother joked that she wishes Andrew's older, straight brother could have found someone like Charles to settle down with.[105]

• Edythe Eyde watched some new neighbors move in — two men, no women. Her suspicions aroused, she went over and said, "Hi. Welcome. I'm your neighbor across the street. I see you have a couple of cats." She played with the cats, then said, "You're gay, aren't you?" The two men were stunned, but she put them at ease by saying, "Well, so am I! Hi, neighbor!" They became good friends and traded jobs as needed. When the gay men went away on business trips, she took care of their cats, and when she needed a difficult-to-replace light bulb changed, they did it for her.[106]

• When comedian Kate Clinton came out to her family as a lesbian, Bill, her brother, decided to tell his children the news. Over dinner, he told them, and Angela, his eleven-year-old daughter, replied, "Well, duh, Dad. I have only known this my entire life."[107]

• Lesbian comedian Judy Carter says that a good way to come out to your friends is to ask, "Are you friends with any gay people?" If they say that they aren't, reply, "Well, you are now."[108]

Gifts

• Quakers are concerned about social justice and about the just distribution of the good things of this world. Long ago, John Cox, Sr., gave hospitality to people travelling west. One guest took a liking to Mr. Cox' son and made him a boat. John Cox, Jr., had only one other toy — a wagon. However, Mr. Cox told his son that he had to give away either the boat or the wagon because as long as there was one child in the world who did not have a toy, he didn't want his son to have two toys.[109]

• When figure skater Dorothy Hamill was 11 years old — in the days before teenagers got their noses pierced as a fashion statement — her friends gave her 13 pairs of earrings. A competition was coming up, and her parents told her that if she won the competition, she could get both ears pierced. However, if she finished second, she could get only one ear pierced, and if she finished third, she could get only her nose pierced.[110]

• At age 13, R.L. Stine received a heavy-duty typewriter as a bar mitzvah gift — a gift he made much use of. During summer vacations in his high school years, he told his parents that he couldn't get a job because he was too busy writing a novel. His parents never questioned this statement. As an adult, Mr. Stein became the author of the *Fear Street* and *Goosebumps* series.[111]

• When American dance pioneers Ted Shawn and Ruth St. Denis married each other, Ms. St. Denis refused to wear a wedding ring because she regarded it as "a symbol of bondage." Later, because Mr. Shawn felt that at least one of them ought to wear a wedding ring, she bought him one as a first-anniversary gift.[112]

• When Giulio Gatti-Casazza was courting soprano Frances Alda, he gave her a perfect lover's gift — a leather-bound volume of love letters he had written to her.[113]

Grandparents

• When Maud Gruss was 12 years old and about to make her first public appearance as a solo tightrope walker, her mother, whose name was Gipsy, showed her a scrapbook filled with photographs and clippings of her own career as a tightrope walker. In one old black-and-white photograph, Maud recognized herself, but Gipsy turned the page, showed her an even older black-and-white photograph, and asked, "And this one, is that you as well?" The young girls in the photographs, although they looked very much like 12-year-old Maud, turned out to be her grandmother Violette and her great-grandmother Germaine, both of whom had been tightrope walkers. (By the way, Maud's public debut went very well, and her father, Alexis, said, "Tonight, a new star is born.")[114]

• George Beatty was a jewelry maker in Cleveland, Ohio. He once received a letter from a wealthy man who wanted him to create a piece of jewelry for the wealthy man's dearest granddaughter. Mr. Beatty noticed that the letter referred to the granddaughter as "dearest" five times, and he prayed to God for inspiration — a prayer that was answered. He created a ring across which were displayed, in order, a diamond, an emerald, an amethyst, a ruby, another emerald, a sapphire, and a topaz. Why are there two emeralds? Mr. Beatty says, "Because there are two e's in 'dearest.' If you take the initials of those stones, it spells the word 'dearest.'"[115]

• As a child, Russian ice skater Ekaterina Gordeeva used to go mushroom hunting with her grandfather. Because all their neighbors also went mushroom hunting, they tried to get up early so they could find mushrooms before anyone else. However, if they were late, her grandfather would tell her not to worry, because their mushrooms would hide from the other mushroom hunters. According to Ms.

Gordeeva, her grandfather was right, because they always found their mushrooms.[116]

• The grandmother of Meredith Willson, author of *The Music Man*, was lying on her deathbed when a truck farmer came by with "triple-strength horseradish guaranteed to grow hair on a china egg." She heard the truck farmer and asked her children to bring her some horseradish and a spoon. She put a spoonful of the horseradish in her mouth, swallowed, then said, "Now there's something with a little character!"[117]

• Fred Rogers, aka Mister Rogers, is named for his grandfather: Fred Brooks McFeely. While Mister Rogers was growing up, his grandfather frequently told him, "I like you, just the way you are." Of course, this is a quotation that he has shared with generations of children who watch his TV show, *Mister Rogers' Neighborhood*.[118]

• One day when he was young, Maury Maverick, Jr., was kissing a girl on his grandmother's front porch, when his grandmother told him to stop that. He replied, "Oh, Grandma, you used to do the same thing back in Virginia behind shutters." His grandmother hit him, then said, "What do you think shutters are for, you young fool?"[119]

• When Ralph Bunche, the first African American to win the Nobel Peace Prize, became valedictorian of his high school in 1922, the principal attempted to compliment him to his grandmother by saying that he never thought of Ralph as a Negro. Ralph's grandmother firmly stated, "He is a Negro — and proud of it."[120]

• Frank DeCaro, the author of *A Boy Named Phyllis*, had a grandmother who liked to read trashy novels such as *Valley of the Dolls* and *Airport* while sitting under a hairdryer. Just to keep her family guessing, however, she occasionally varied her reading matter with a book such as *Saints to Know and Love*.[121]

• Jayree, one of Jerry Clower's grandsons, came to visit his grandparents for a while, and Homerline, his grandmother, told him a couple of times to pick up his toys. Jayree ignored her for a while, then he put his hands on his hips and asked Mr. Clower, "Grandaddy, how have you lived with her all these years?"[122]

• Famed conductor Arturo Toscanini asked his granddaughter Sonia Horowitz, whose father was the famed pianist Vladimir Horowitz, whether she would prefer to be a conductor like her grandfather or a pianist like her father. She answered, "A conductor — because it's a lot easier."[123]

• When television talk-show host David Letterman was a small child, his grandfather used to take him out to hunt for watermelons. They were always careful to sneak up on the watermelons, because if a watermelon knows you are coming, it will run away.[124]

Halloween

• When ballerina Darci Kistler was five years old, a neighbor gave her a Halloween costume — a pink tutu. Because she knew that she wanted to learn to dance (even at age three, she was cutting photographs of ballerinas out of magazines), she wore the tutu around the house after Halloween as a hint for her mother to sign her up for dance lessons. The hint worked.[125]

Husbands and Wives

• Just after the end of World War II, while country comedian Archie Campbell was still an enlisted man in the United States Navy, he hadn't seen his wife for a long time, so he asked Lieutenant Sam Bailey if a way could be arranged for him to see her. Therefore, Lieutenant Bailey asked Mr. Campbell to take an apparatus to Florida to have it repaired — of course, Mr. Campbell had his wife meet him in Florida. At the repair shop, Mr. Campbell asked how long it would take to have the apparatus repaired, and the technician assured him that it would be repaired by the very next day. This was bad news for Mr. Campbell and his wife, so he explained the situation to the technician, saying, "I haven't seen my wife in over a year. Take longer than that." The technician replied, "In that case, it will take at least a week."[126]

• As a world-class track athlete, Thelma Wright competed away from home, meaning long separations from her husband, Lee. And even when her husband was nearby, practices, competitions, and media interviews sometimes kept her from seeing him. At the 1972 Olympic Games, many fans asked for her autograph and gave her pieces of papers to sign. While she was surrounded by autograph-seeking fans one day, someone gave her a crumpled piece of paper. She looked up to see who had given her the paper — it was her husband, who said, "Hi, I just wanted to say hello."[127]

• Hugh Downs and his wife were in Washington, D.C. While Mr. Downs' wife was in the shower, he received a telephone call saying that their flight to New York had been cancelled because of bad weather. However, after making a telephone call, he discovered that a train would be leaving soon for New York. So he quickly packed all of his and his wife's clothing and had it sent to the train station. Just then, his wife came into the bedroom with a towel wrapped around her. "Dear," she said, "would you please hand me my green dress?"[128]

• A housewife once bought some guest towels for a party. She hung them up in the bathroom, but being afraid that her husband would use the towels before the party started, she hung a sign on them: "If you use these towels, I'll kill you." Then she went around the house, making other preparations. The party seemed to go well, but when it was over, she noticed that none of the guests had used the guest towels — she had forgotten to take down the sign.[129]

• When Constance Samwell was secretly engaged to Frank Benson, she sometimes heard two actresses discussing in the dressing room which of them would marry him. Sometimes, one of the actresses would say that Mr. Benson had walked her home and stayed with her until late — but Ms. Samwell knew that Mr. Benson had walked her home that particular night and stayed with her until late. (Later, Constance and Frank were married.)[130]

• Jane Stevenson learned that her police officer husband was a transvestite on their wedding night. He came out of the bathroom wearing a white embroidered peignoir that was prettier than what she was wearing. On his face was an imploring look that said, "Please understand me." She put her arms around him, and she said, "I love you." He said, "I can't help this." She replied, "You don't have to explain. I love you. Tonight you don't have to explain. I accept it."[131]

• In his old age, Moe Howard of Three Stooges fame guested on TV's *Mike Douglas Show*. At one point, Mr. Douglas asked Moe if he had "any unfulfilled ambitions." Moe got a gleam in his eye, grabbed a pie (when you're a Stooge, one is always handy), charged straight into the audience, and hit his wife smack in the face with the pie. His wife, Helen, took it well, saying, "Moe's been rehearsing for that all his life. I'm glad he finally got it out of his system."[132]

• In the 16th century, Irishwoman Elizabeth Fitzgerald was surrounded by enemies who told her that they had captured her husband and would hang him unless she surrendered her castle immediately. Standing on the battlements of her castle, Ms. Fitzgerald shouted, "Mark these words — they may serve your own wives on some occasion. I'll keep my castle; for Elizabeth Fitzgerald may get another husband, but Elizabeth Fitzgerald may never get another castle."[133]

• Henny Youngman's most famous joke was written by accident. One day, he was preparing for a stint on the Kate Smith radio show, when his wife and some of her friends came backstage to visit him. Unfortunately, because of their talking, Mr. Youngman wasn't able to concentrate on his preparation, so he decided to have someone take his wife and her friends to sit in the audience. Finding a stagehand, he told him, "Take my wife — please![134]

• Israel Zangwill married a non-Jew in 1901, upsetting many Jews. Shortly after his marriage, he spoke before a large Jewish audience. Worried about how his wife would be treated, he said to the audience, "Fellow Jews, I trust you will be courteous to Mrs. Zangwill, and that you will not do or say anything that might offend her. While I may deserve censure for marrying a Gentile, Mrs. Zangwill deserves nothing but praise — she married a Jew."[135]

• Elizabeth Barrett Browning's *Sonnets from the Portuguese* were poems intended to be read only by her husband, Robert Browning, but because of their high quality, he insisted that they be published. The sonnets were not translated from Portuguese. Instead, the poems received this particular title because Mr. Browning called his wife, who had a dark complexion, "my little Portuguese."[136]

• When African-American comedian Dick Gregory became a stand-up comedian, he knew that eventually someone in the audience would call him a n*gger, so he practiced controlling his reaction by having his wife yell "n*gger" at him at home. When it finally happened in a nightclub, Mr. Gregory had his response ready: "You hear what that guy just called me? Roy Rogers' horse. He called me Trigger."[137]

• Mark Twain liked to visit neighbors informally — without wearing a collar or tie. This upset his wife, Livy, so Mr. Twain wrapped up a package which he sent to his neighbors along with this note: "A little while ago, I visited you for about half an hour minus my collar and tie. The missing articles are enclosed. Will you kindly gaze at them for 30 minutes and then return them to me?"[138]

• Anne Sexton once wrote a volume of poetry titled *Love Poems*. One poem was intended to be titled "Twenty-One Days Without You" because her career required her to spend that amount of time away from her husband. However, the title had to be changed to "Eighteen Days Without You" after her husband said to her, "I can't stand it any longer; you haven't been with me for days."[139]

• Robert Dole and his wife, Elizabeth, once made the bed while posing for *People* magazine. When the photographs were published, a man wrote Senator Dole, complaining that he was making things tough for men all over the country. Senator Dole wrote back, "You don't know the half of it. The only reason she was helping was because they were taking pictures."[140]

• Journalist Heywood Broun met and married Ruth Hale, who was also a journalist. On their first date, they walked in the park, where a squirrel came up to them and begged for food. Ms. Hale told Mr. Broun that she wished she had some nuts for the squirrel, and Mr. Broun replied, "I can't help you except to give him a nickel so he can go and buy his own."[141]

• Donald Grey Barnhouse, a pastor, once stayed at the house of an Australian man who had married an American woman. Before the two were married, the woman had never allowed her future husband to kiss her, so their first kiss took place before the altar of the church. "But," said her husband, "after I got the first one, the rest came easy."[142]

• Terence Grey, the owner of a British theater, once heard that his wife was having an affair. He rushed home, grabbed an axe, used it to beat his way through the bedroom door, and stood with the axe raised in front of the bed, on which lay his cowering wife and her cowering lover. Then he lowered the axe and stuck out his tongue at them.[143]

• The wife of Albert Einstein, the great physicist and mathematician, once toured the Mt. Wilson Observatory in California, where her tour guide explained that all this expensive, modern equipment was being used to "find out the shape of the universe." Mrs. Einstein replied, "Oh, my husband does that on the back of an old envelope."[144]

• Harry Belafonte talked about his family while he was on *The Mike Douglas Show*, mentioning that his oldest child was 24 years old. When Mike Douglas asked how long he had been married, he answered, "Seventeen years." Mr. Douglas began to count on his fingers, and Mr. Belafonte added, "Hey, I've been married before."[145]

• Rusty Kothavala was a proctor and instructor at Harvard. After getting married and fathering a daughter, he discovered he was gay and began frequenting gay bars. When he eventually told his wife, she was very understanding: "Is that all? Here I thought you were one of these international criminals or something."[146]

• During World War I, dancer Ted Shawn joined the United States Army. His wife, Ruth St. Denis, performed for the troops and then the next day watched a parade in which her husband took part. When Ms. St. Denis was asked what she thought of the parade, she replied, "Oh, I thought *he* was grand."[147]

• Mark Twain enjoyed reading and writing in bed. One day, a reporter was coming over to interview him, so his wife, Livy, said, "Don't you think it would be a bit embarrassing for the reporter — your being in bed?" Mr. Twain replied, "Why, Livy, if you think so, we might have the other bed made up for him."[148]

• Anna Pavlova, in addition to being a dancer, was also a wife. People going backstage at the New York Metropolitan Opera House were once treated to the sight of Ms. Pavlova throwing ballet slippers at the back of her retreating husband, Victor Dandré, while she shouted at him in Russian.[149]

• Stand-up comedian Rita Rudner used to do a lot of jokes about being single, and when she got married, she worried about losing 20 minutes of comic material. Still, she was glad she got married. In fact, she says, "For him, I would have given up 40 minutes."[150]

• Jack Gilford's wife, Madeline, had been married before. She remained married for eight years, then got a divorce. On his 8th anniversary, Mr. Gilford told a friend, "I better run home and see if my option has been picked up."[151]

Chapter 4: From Illness to Parents

Illness

• Mister Rogers really did answer his fan mail — as is shown by the book *Dear Mister Rogers, Does It Ever Rain in Your Neighborhood?* One letter was from a mother whose daughter, Michelle — only five-and-a-half years old — needed radiation treatment for an inoperable brain tumor. Michelle refused to undergo the treatment because she had to be alone, even though the treatment would last just one minute. After a few days of refusing the treatment, Michelle asked, "What's a minute?" Her mother answered by singing part of Mister Rogers' theme song, "It's a Beautiful Day in the Neighborhood," and said, "Oops! The minute is up. I can't even finish Mister Rogers' song." Michelle then exclaimed, "Is that a minute? I can do that!" — and did.[152]

• While researching a book on children surviving cancer, Erma Bombeck was impressed by the way a three-year-old boy faced life. The boy told her, "You know what? I'm going to the circus!" — but a camp counselor reminded the boy that he wasn't going to the circus, but he was going swimming instead. The boy then turned to Ms. Bombeck and said, "You know what? I'm going swimming!" Ms. Bombeck wrote later, "It didn't matter, he would have gone to the opening of a bottle of aspirin. And it made me think — little things, little moments. Go for them."[153]

• Albert III, Al Gore's six-year-old son, was hit by a car in 1989 and thrown for several feet, breaking some of his bones and crushing some of his internal organs. He was rushed to a hospital, and when he regained consciousness, he told his parents, "I can't get well without you." They stayed with him throughout his three-week hospital stay, and when they took him home in a full-body cast, they put a bed for him in the dining room and took turns sleeping on a mattress placed on the floor by his bed until he recovered.[154]

• Many people fear AIDS. Carmine Buete was a 10-year-old boy suffering from AIDS who lived with his grandmother near New Year City. After some of the friends of his grandmother discovered that he had AIDS, they refused to talk to her anymore. Because of that experience, Carmine and his grandmother soon learned not to tell many people that he had AIDS. Before he died, one of Carmine's favorite toys was an E.T. doll that made him feel better when he was ill.[155]

• Teddy Kennedy, Jr., the senator's son, lost a leg to cancer in 1973. He used humor to deal with his prosthesis (artificial limb). While he was riding on the back of a friend's bicycle, they crashed, and young Ted's foot became twisted around backwards. No problem. He simply twisted his foot around so it was facing the right way, then he walked away. The people watching him — who didn't know he was wearing a prosthesis — were shocked.[156]

In-Laws

• Mark Twain married a woman from a wealthy family. Arriving in Buffalo, New York, Mr. and Mrs. Twain were driven to a fancy house, where his new wife told Mr. Twain that the fancy house was a gift to them from her father. Mr. Twain shook hands with his father-in-law and said, "If you ever come to Buffalo, bring your grip [suitcase] and stay all night — it won't cost you a cent."[157]

• A 1993 TV commercial for a Norwegian airline showed a man stripping until he was wearing nothing but his socks, then bursting through a doorway to surprise his wife. Unfortunately, her parents are with her — and they know don't where to look. The title card for the commercial says, "Warning: we're flying in your in-laws at half-price."[158]

• Irish ballad writer Jimmy Hiney is a small man. When he was first introduced to his mother-in-law, she told her daughter, "Well, by God, if you get nothing else from him, you'll always get a laugh."[159]

Language

• As the writer of most episodes of *The Twilight Zone*, host Rod Serling displayed a love of language, a love that he exhibited even as a child. When he was six years old, his family took a two-and-a-half-hour car trip from Binghamton, New York, to Syracuse, New York. Before the trip, his parents agreed that they would not speak until young Rod had stopped talking. However, they never got a chance to speak during the trip because Rod never stopped talking![160]

• After being divorced from his father, Zack's mother, Aimee, discovered that she was in love with another woman, Margie, and they moved in together. Zack occasionally hears other people use words such as "fag" and "dyke," but his mother tells him, "The problem is not with us. It's with them. We're in a family where everybody loves each other, and that's what matters."[161]

Money

• Wilson Mizner once married a rich society lady, which seemed to be a marriage made in Heaven, given Mr. Mizner's great delight in spending money. However, his wife kept a tight grip on her money, giving her husband very little of it. Mr. Mizner once got on his knees and pleaded for an hour with his wife to prove her love for him by signing a blank check, but she would not. While dining at the Waldorf-Astoria, Mr. Mizner was again pleading for money. This so annoyed his wife that she began beating him with the nearest thing she had in her possession — an envelope filled with money. The envelope came open, the money spilled everywhere, and Mr. Mizner and the other diners in the restaurant began scrambling for it. His wife saw him on his knees, picking up money, and screamed that he could have the money since he was willing to crawl for it. Mr. Mizner said later, "I'd picked up $8,000 before I realized I'd been insulted."[162]

• When Pulitzer Prize-winning reporter Meyer Berger was a boy, his family was poor in money. One day early in the 20th century, he announced to his mother that he had been given the honor of making an acceptance speech because a local organization was donating a new flag to his school. Of course, this was good news, but his mother looked at his shoes and was embarrassed. She told the family that they had only 25 cents, and either she could use the money to buy Meyer a used pair of shoes so he could be decently dressed when he made the acceptance speech, or she could put it in the gas meter and the family could eat a hot supper. The family voted for the shoes, and they ate a cold supper that night. After young Meyer had made his acceptance speech at school, he repeated it at home so his family could hear him.[163]

• Author Donald Ogden Stewart's son once broke a window. Since Mr. Stewart had to go to work at a movie studio on a Sunday, he tried to use the occasion to make his son feel guilty for breaking the window by saying that Daddy had to go to work to pay for the broken window instead of playing tennis, as he had hoped. Mr. Stewart asked his son, "Aren't you sorry that poor, dear Daddy has to work on his day off, just because of you?" His son replied, "If you have any money left over, buy me an air rifle."[164]

• When Eugene Field was a student at Knox College, he sometimes telegraphed his guardian, Melvin L. Gray, for money. If the requested money was slow in arriving, Mr. Field would telegraph Mr. Gray again, saying that unless he received some money quickly, he would be forced to go into show business and bill himself as "Melvin L. Gray, Banjo and Specialty Artist."[165]

• In 1934, Will Rogers starred in *Ah, Wilderness*, a play by Eugene O'Neill. However, after he received a letter from a minister telling him that this particular play was unsuitable for being seen by families, Mr. Rogers declined to star in the movie version of the play, thereby losing a salary of over $200,000 — a sum that is approximately $2 million in year 2000 money.[166]

Mothers
• George Burns loved his mother and regarded her as a wonderful problem-solver. For example, when one of his sisters, Mamie, and her husband, Dr. Max Salis, were having problems and considering getting

a divorce, his mother called in her daughter and listened to her side of the story. Then she told her daughter, "Mamie, you're wrong and the doctor is right. I want you to apologize to Max. Tell him you're sorry and that it won't happen again." After Mamie had left, his mother called in Max and told him, "Doctor, Mamie was right. Don't ever do that again."[167]

• Faye Zealand, as part of the AIDS Resource Foundation for Children, has much experience not only with children who have HIV or AIDS, but also with children whose parents have died from AIDS. She knows one little girl who wanted a photograph of her mother, who had died from AIDS. Her foster mother got her a photo, but other people were in it, and the little girl asked for a photo showing only her mother. After she received this photo, the little girl would put it on top of her pillow at night, placing it so that it touched her head — only then would she go to sleep.[168]

• When David Letterman is in Indiana, he visits his mother. One day, he called his mother to let her know he was coming over, and when he arrived at her house, she asked him, "David, would you like some strawberry pie?" He saw a freshly baked strawberry pie on a table, so he asked her, "When did you make this?" She replied, "I started right after I got off the phone with you." Mr. Letterman was pleased: "It was just the cutest. I was so touched. Isn't that motherhood? She gets off the phone, drops what she's doing, and *bakes a pie*."[169]

• When Olympic-gold-medal gymnast Bart Conner and his brothers were growing up, they had a lot of gymnastics equipment, including a set of parallel bars in the basement and a set of rings in the yard. Their mother was afraid they would hurt themselves, so occasionally she would drive around looking for discarded mattresses the day before the trash was picked up. When she found one, she would ask if she could have it, and she would take it home and place it under the gymnastics equipment.[170]

• As a single mother, Mary Jane Kurtz found it difficult to get her children ready on time to go to church. One Sunday morning, she told her children to get ready in no uncertain terms and they started laughing at her. They told her, "Mom, every time you slam down your foot, smoke comes out. It must be the wrath of God!" The smoke was actually the powder she had put in her shoes, but thereafter her children got ready on time to go to church.[171]

• Twyla Tharp's mother had great faith in her daughter. Whenever Twyla brought home a report card that carried any grade lower than an A-, her mother immediately assumed that her daughter's teacher was incompetent and made arrangements for Twyla to attend a different class — and sometimes a different school. Later, Twyla became the world-famous choreographer of *Push Comes to Shove*.[172]

• English entertainer Joyce Grenfell was an actress who played a series of unglamorous roles in the movies, disappointing her mother, who wanted Joyce to be glamorous. Once, her mother told a friend that her daughter was in a movie that they were going to see, but when she saw Joyce in yet another unglamorous role, she told her friend that she had been mistaken and her daughter wasn't in the movie.[173]

• Comedian W.C. Fields was good to his mother. After leaving home, he studied juggling and comedy. Once he began to make good, he sent his mother a note and a $10 bill in December of 1898, and thereafter he sent her at least $10 a week. However, in keeping with his comic persona, he didn't let people know what he was doing, and he always denied that he would ever help his family.[174]

• Parents sometimes are shocked to learn that one of their children is gay, but often they quickly adjust — usually after spending some time wondering whether they caused their child's homosexuality. One mother went through that process, but eventually joked to her gay son, "I finally figured out why you are gay — I chewed Juicy Fruit gum while I was pregnant with you."[175]

• As part of the Kinaaldá ceremony that marks a Navajo girl's coming of age, the girl's mother "molds" her with her hands into the shape of a beautiful and strong woman. When Celinda McKelvey's mother molded her, she squeezed her stomach "so you don't grow up to be fat." Smiling, Celinda asked her mother to do it again — "just to make sure I stay skinny."[176]

• Eve Arden appeared in a play titled *The Road to Rome*, about the Carthaginian general Hannibal. Once, when Hannibal's soldiers roughly dragged Ms. Arden's character away on stage, the voice of Liza, Ms. Arden's two-year-old daughter, could be heard in the audience, asking, "What are those men doing to my mommy?"[177]

• When author Frank DeCaro's mother decided to learn to drive, she asked her brother to teach her. He immediately drove his car to the top of the steepest hill in town, got himself and his dog out of the car, then told her, "Go ahead. Drive." Decades later, she still complained, "Can you believe he took his dog with him?"[178]

• When comedian Bob Smith came out to his mother, she said, "You're gay ... well, it could be worse. Look at the Gardiners across the street with those retarded grandchildren." Mr. Smith laughed and said, "Thanks, Mom. I love that comparison." Shortly afterward, she wrote him a loving letter of acceptance.[179]

• As a young boy, Bart Conner was already into gymnastics. Often, he used to come home from school, and talk to his mother while he was standing on his head. Once, while he was standing on his head, she stood on *her* head and they talked to each other.[180]

• Figure skater Peggy Fleming keeps scrapbooks filled with photographs of her family and children in a cabinet near her garage door. Why? If her house is ever threatened by fire, she wants her photographs handy so she can save them.[181]

Music

• Before her marriage, soprano Frances Alda had many beaus. Once, four of her beaus showed up on the same day to hear her perform at the Metropolitan Opera. Each beau told her where he would be sitting at the Met. During the course of the opera, Ms. Alda sang in turn to each part of the Met where she knew one of her beaus would be sitting. By the time the opera was over, she had convinced each beau that she had been singing especially to him.[182]

• Ballerina Suzanne Farrell and her choreographer husband, Paul Mejia, bought an island in a lake in the Adirondack Mountains and turned it into a dance camp. Often, local tourist boats would cruise past the island, which the tour guides called "Ballerina Island." A nearby local couple ate their dinners during the early ballet class so they could enjoy the romantic music.[183]

• John von Neumann was a child prodigy, but not in music. His parents made him take music lessons, but they were surprised at his lack of improvement. Then they discovered that as their son practiced music scales on his cello, he was reading a science or history book that he had placed on his music stand.[184]

Old Age

• Paul Douglas used to be a United States senator. When he was old, he suffered a stroke and was confined to a wheelchair. One day, while reaching for something, he fell out of his wheelchair. The only other person at home was his wife, who wasn't strong enough to pick him up and put him back in the wheelchair. She told her husband, "Paul, we haven't had a picnic in such a long time," then she went into the kitchen and made some sandwiches. She brought out the sandwiches, put a few potted plants around to make the scene look more like the country, and opened a bottle of wine. The two had their picnic, and then they read love poetry to each other until someone arrived to help pick up Mr. Douglas.[185]

• An aged parent had a problem, so he asked R' Shmuel Salant for advice. The problem was this: His sons had moved to America, and now they did not keep the Sabbath or observe the other commandments that God had given His chosen people. However, his sons did send him money, and he worried whether it was proper to accept the money. R' Shmuel Salant said, "Your sons wish to keep only one commandment, that of honoring their parents, and you wish to deprive them of that as well?"[186]

• All his life, Rabbi Moshe Feinstein got up each day at 4 a.m. in order to study. When he was 85, his wife pleaded with him to get up a little later, so that he could rest more, but he replied that he needed to get up that early to study because he didn't want to remain an ignoramus.[187]

Olympics

• United States figure skater Tara Lipinski has wanted to win a medal at the Olympics ever since she was a child. When she was still a toddler, the Olympics were on TV, but she didn't pay much attention until some medals were awarded — then she was fascinated. She watched the athletes stand on podiums, wearing ribbons around their necks and holding flowers. Tara's parents used to keep her toys in Tupperware containers, so to create a podium, she turned over one of the Tupperware containers and stood on it, then she asked her mother for a ribbon and some flowers so she could be like the athletes on TV.[188]

• Strange things sometimes happen to child athletes. When she was nine years old, Russian figure skater Ekaterina Gordeeva began to skate in a competition, but she discovered that she could not move her head because she had accidentally zipped her hair in her costume. She had to stop skating so she could unzip her ponytail. As an adult, she won two Olympic gold medals in pairs skating with her husband, Sergei Grinkov.[189]

• As a young gymnast, Dominic Moceanu showed a lot of confidence. While signing autographs before the 1996 Olympic Games in Atlanta were held, she added to her signature, "'96 gold, for sure." Her cockiness was justified — the United States women's gymnastics team, of which Ms. Moceanu was a member, won the gold medal.[190]

• After Dorothy Hamill won the gold medal in women's figure skating at the 1976 Olympic Games, she slept with it under her pillow. The next day, someone asked where she was keeping it. She pulled it from out of her blouse and said, "Right here."[191]

Parents

• Tara Lipinski is a champion figure skater, but her parents had to sacrifice for her to become a champion. Her father lived in Texas, where his job is, but Tara and her mother lived in Detroit, where she could train with a top coach and skate at a top rink. In addition, her parents refinanced their house and took out a loan to pay for Tara's skating, coaching, and travel expenses. Now that Tara is an Olympic gold medalist and a professional figure skater, she earns enough money by performing to more than pay for her expenses. (The parents of many other champion sports stars also make these kinds of sacrifices.)[192]

• Zack lives in New Jersey and has same-sex parents — Aimee and Margie. One day, he was talking with his friend Alex and they stopped talking when Zack's mother and her lover — Zack calls them his two mothers — walked up to them. Curious, Zack's mother, Aimee, asked what was going on. Alex replied, "I wanted to know if it's all right if I told someone that you're a lesbian." Aimee looked at Margie for a moment, then the two women laughed, and Aimee said, "Sure, it's all right. We like being lesbians."[193]

• Parents worry about their teenage children going out on dates, and they want to meet the people their children are dating. A mother was shocked when her daughter said she was going on a date with a boy the mother had not met, so the girl's mother decided to call the boy's mother to find out something about him. The boy's mother stated, "He's my son, and I love him." Hearing that, the girl's mother sighed and said, "Well, that's fine. I'm sure everything will be all right."[194]

• Some teachers can get upset with parents. Following one conference with a mother, a Quaker teacher exclaimed, "The only people who ought not to have children are parents!" A former head of

Bootham School, a school for Quakers, once said, "There are moments when I feel that in the next world I would like to be Head Master of an orphanage."[195]

• When Mexican artist Diego Rivera was a small child, he liked to draw on walls and furniture. Of course, his parents didn't want him to do this, but they did want him to use his creativity, so his father set aside an entire room for young Diego. He covered the entire room with canvas, so Diego was able to draw wherever he liked in that room.[196]

• When children compete at important sports events, their parents react in different ways. When Dorothy Hamill won the gold medal in women's figure skating at the 1976 Olympic Games, her father watched the competition in person, but her mother was too nervous to watch and stayed in her hotel room.[197]

• Etiquette expert Grace Fox knows a family that schedules regular musical or literary nights. On one occasion, the parents tried to turn on their children — metalheads all — to the music of the Beatles and Janis Joplin. (Their children remained metalheads, but everyone had fun.)[198]

• When he was growing up, professional baseball player Harmon Killebrew used to play ball with his brother and father in the front yard. His mother once complained that they were ruining the lawn, but his father replied, "We're raising kids — not raising grass."[199]

• Trevor Mark Sage-EL is a bi-racial child growing up in New Jersey. His father is black, and his mother is white. When people ask Trevor what he is, he replies, "Human." And when he thinks it is necessary, he asks, "What are you? Alien?"[200]

Chapter 5: From Physicians to Work

Physicians

• Leila Denmark, born 1898, was still practicing pediatric medicine at age 100. Her advice often drew on her long experience in life. Once, a mother called Dr. Denmark after her two children had gotten pinworm. Dr. Denmark told her that it wasn't anything to worry about and to bring the children to her clinic on Monday. Then Dr. Denmark asked why the mother was crying. After learning that she was crying because her husband was blaming her for the children's contracting pinworm, Dr. Denmark made a prescription: "You go gather the family up, and everybody go on a picnic today."[201]

• A man was doing minor repairs around the house, and he decided to revarnish the toilet seat. Unfortunately, he forgot to tell his wife, and a short time later, he heard her calling from the bathroom, "I'm stuck!" Unable to free his wife, the man unbolted the toilet seat and carried both her and it to the bedroom, where he placed her face down on the bed, then called their physician. The physician arrived, surveyed the situation, then said, "I agree that it's very pretty, but why did you decide to frame it?"[202]

Practical Jokes

• When Al Gore was appearing on the TV program *Larry King Live*, his wife, Tipper, phoned in and, disguising her voice, said, "I just had to tell you — you're the most handsome man I've ever seen." Still disguising her voice, she asked him for a date. Mr. Gore didn't recognize her voice, so he was embarrassed as he tried to stammer out an answer. Finally, Mr. King pointed out that Mr. Gore was a married man and so of course he wouldn't be willing to make a date. Using her own voice, Mrs. Gore then asked, "Not even with his wife?"[203]

• Comedian Robin Williams' mother had a sense of humor. She once attended an invitational dance at the Lake Forest — Lake Bluff (Illinois) Bath and Tennis Club. She dressed extremely well, but she also blacked out her front teeth, making herself appear toothless. All around her, people were saying, "You'd think someone who could afford clothes like that could afford to get her teeth fixed."[204]

• Beatrice Kaufman once asked Alexander Woollcott to write a reference letter so her daughter could attend a certain school. As a joke, Mr. Woollcott sent to Mrs. Kaufman what she took to be a carbon copy of his reference letter, which began: "I implore you to accept this unfortunate child and remove her from her shocking environment."[205]

Prejudice

• As a bi-racial child, Trevor Mark Sage-EL is aware of racism. His father is black, and his mother is white. When his parents needed a loan to buy a house, they went together to a bank, where their loan application was turned down. So the next time his mother went alone to the bank, and this time their loan application was accepted. Trevor also is aware that his family is treated differently when he is alone with his father than when he is alone with his mother. Once, a woman thought that his father, who was eating a hamburger, was going to steal her purse. That kind of thing doesn't happen when Trevor is alone with his mother.[206]

• Families change. Two parents discovered that their young son was gay, and they took the news so badly that their son ran away for a year. They were overwhelmed with remorse and did their best to track their son down. Eventually, they discovered that he was in Portland, Oregon, so they went to the police there for help, but the woman police officer the father first contacted immediately told him that homosexuality is wrong. The father told her, "I don't give a d*mn how you feel about it. This is my son and I need to find him — he's 15 years old."[207]

Problem-Solving

• A couple of American teachers who were best friends went on a trip to Mexico. Walking along a street, they were arrested and taken to the police station, where they discovered that they had been walking in a red-light district in which the only women allowed were licensed prostitutes. The fine for a woman without a prostitute's license walking there was 20,000 pesos. Like most teachers, the women didn't have much money, and what money they did have, they wanted to spend on their vacation, not on a fine. Fortunately, they found a way out of their dilemma: In order not to spend good money on a fine, and with no thought of taking up a new profession, each teacher avoided the fine by purchasing a prostitute's license for 20 pesos.[208]

• When he was a child, John W. Mauchly liked to read in bed at night, but his mother wanted him to get his sleep, so she sometimes checked to make sure that his light was out. Therefore, he invented a special lamp to solve this problem. When his mother came up the stairs to check on him, the lamp automatically went out. When she went down the stairs after checking up on him, the lamp automatically came on again. As an adult, Mr. Mauchly became one of the co-designers of the ENIAC and UNIVAC computers.[209]

• Buddy and Vilma Ebsen were a famous brother-and-sister dance team during the 1930s. They danced to arrangements by Glenn Miller, who put a lot of brass into the arrangements. Sometimes, the brass players in small towns would object to playing the arrangements, so Buddy would ask his sister, "Would you go give them your brass-section smile?"[210]

• Comedian Joe E. Brown's household was filled with milk drinkers — they drank 17 quarts a day. Because so many milk drinkers were in the family, there often wasn't any left for Mr. Brown to have a glass late at night after returning home from work. His wife solved the problem by putting the sign "POISON — DON'T DRINK" on one bottle each day.[211]

Public Speaking

• William Jennings Bryan ran for President of the United States against William F. McKinley. While on the campaign trail, Mr. Bryan made a speech in which he told his audience that "come November, my wife will be sleeping in the White House." A man in the crowd immediately yelled, "And if she is, she'll be sleeping with McKinley."[212]

• The unmarried daughter of English statesman William Wilberforce campaigned for him. As she rose to speak, the audience chanted, "Miss Wilberforce forever! Miss Wilberforce forever!" She replied, "I thank you, gentlemen, but I do not wish to remain *Miss* Wilberforce forever."[213]

Sex

• A 1991 public service TV commercial in Spain showed a high school principal snooping in the locker rooms as students take gym class. The principal walks into the gym, holds a condom up high, and tells the students in a threatening voice, "I found this in your locker room. Whose is it?" A boy says, "It's mine." Instantly, another boy says, "It's mine." Then a girl says, "It's mine." Suddenly, dozens of students, all of whom resent the principal's snooping, are telling the principal, "It's mine." At this point comes the public service message: "The condom is the most efficient method for preventing unwanted births and sexually transmitted diseases. Put it on. Put it on him."[214]

• As you would expect, Groucho Marx was very good at puncturing the pride of rich people. During World War II, so many men were away fighting that Groucho was forced to do his own gardening. A rich woman saw him, assumed that he was a real gardener, and tried to entice him away from the family that she supposed had hired him. She stopped her car and asked, "Oh, gardener — how much do you get a month?" Groucho replied, "Oh, I don't get paid in dollars — the lady of the house lets me sleep with her." (Of course, Groucho was married to the lady of his house.)[215]

• A wealthy man once walked in his garden, where he saw his gardener and the gardener's beautiful wife. Because the wealthy man wanted to sleep with the gardener's beautiful wife, he sent the gardener on an errand, then told the gardener's wife to shut all the gates of the garden. However, the gardener's wife knew what he was up to, so when she returned, she told him, "I have shut all the gates but one." The wealthy man asked, "Which gate is that?" She replied, "The gate that is between us and God." After hearing her answer, the wealthy man begged her to forgive him.[216]

• A couple of professors at the University of Washington were immensely cool. On their table was prominently displayed a copy of Masters and Johnson's *Human Sexual Response*, which reported the results of their research on sex. Inside was an inscription written by Masters and Johnson themselves: "Thanks for your cooperation."[217]

Siblings

• Buddy Ebsen is perhaps best known for portraying the character of Jed Clampett in the TV series *The Beverly Hillbillies*; however, he and Vilma Ebsen were a popular brother-and-sister dance team in the 1930s. As they toured, their billing changed frequently. Sometimes they were billed as the Ebsens, but at other times they were billed as Vilma and Buddy Ebsen. However, Vilma was upset once when they were billed in two towns in a row as "Buddy Ebsen and Sister Vilma." She even threatened, "If that is not replaced with Vilma and Buddy Ebsen, or The Ebsens, you will be very interested to know that I'm doing the whole act in a nun's habit. If I'm going to be Sister Vilma, then I'll be 'Sister' Vilma!"[218]

• Fortunately, homosexuality is becoming more accepted. Lesbian comedian Kate Clinton was trying to get into a concert featuring Ellen DeGeneres when she had to ask a police officer for help. The police officer asked her a few questions — then he tried to fix her up with his sister![219]

• Quaker William H. Sessions once heard a woman in the Salvation Army say that when she realized that wearing jewelry would cause her to go to hell, she immediately gathered up all her jewelry — and gave it to her sister![220]

• Early in figure skater Rudy Galindo's career, he was financially supported by Laura, his sister. For a while, he affectionately called her the "Bank of Laura."[221]

Sons

• Yitta Halberstam Mandelbaum used to tell bedtime stories to Eli, her son. For an entire year, each of the bedtime stories she told was about her rabbi, Shlomo Carlebach! Eventually, she collected the stories into a book that her son urged her to title *The Rabbi of Love*. (She used the title *Holy Brother*.) Here is one story she tells in the book: In the early 1980s, Rabbi Carlebach, aka the Singing Rabbi, gave a concert to a maximum-security prison for both Jewish and Arab women in Ramlah, Israel. However, when the concert was scheduled to begin, Rabbi Shlomo noticed that only Jewish prisoners were present, so he asked that the Arab prisoners also attend his concert. By the end of the concert, everyone—Jewish prisoners, Arab prisoners, and prison guards—were singing together and dancing in a circle.[222]

• A Jew met a cantor and asked, "What shall I do? My son has decided to convert to Christianity." The cantor replied, "Funny you should ask — my son has also decided to convert." Together they sought their rabbi and asked, "What shall we do? Our sons have decided to convert to Christianity." The rabbi replied, "Funny you should ask — my son has also decided to convert." Together they decided to pray to God: "What shall we do? Our sons have decided to convert to Christianity." Out of Heaven, a mighty voice replied, "Funny you should ask ...."[223]

• Poet Nikki Giovanni read frequently to Thomas, her young son, but occasionally she was tired and told him, "Go read it yourself," although he was too young to read. One day, she said that to him, and he replied, "OK, I will." Ms. Giovanni said, "But you don't know how to read." However, Thomas proved that he could read by picking up a *New York Times* and reading the headlines out loud to her. Immediately, Ms. Giovanni read a story to him. She explained later, "I didn't want to punish him for having learned to read, by not reading to him."[224]

• Francis Hodgson Burnett, author of *A Little Princess* and *The Secret Garden*, based the title character of her novel *Little Lord Fauntleroy* on her own son, Vivien. In 1937, Vivien Burnett died a hero. Two men and two women were in a craft that overturned in a sound. Vivien maneuvered his yawl to the overturned craft and rescued the two men and two women, then he collapsed and died.[225]

• Comedian Robin Williams often watched Saturday morning cartoons with Zach, his young son. While watching, Mr. Williams sometimes did funny voices and made funny remarks. Usually, Zach enjoyed this, but sometimes he told his father, "Daddy, don't use that voice. Just be Daddy."[226]

• One day, Bobbie, Beatrice Lillie's son, came in the house after playing in the garden. Ms. Lillie saw the dirt on her son's face and arms and asked what he had been doing. He said, "I've been in the garden playing with the faeries." She replied, "Faeries? Elves, dear."[227]

• Jack, Art Linkletter's son, attended Beverly Hills High School, where he once ran for class president. Because 85 percent of the school's students were Jewish, Jack used the name "Linkletterberg" for campaigning purposes and almost won the election.[228]

Thanksgiving

• According to Totie Fields, her sister (Rosie), was the best cook in the family. Just before one Thanksgiving, Rosie prepared a feast of Jewish dishes — mushroom and barley soup, noodle pudding, brisket, and so on. (Totie says that this is what the Jewish Pilgrims ate.) Because the refrigerator and freezer were already full, they carried the Thanksgiving food out to the garage and left it there, knowing that the weather was cold enough to keep the food safe. Thanksgiving morning they went to the garage, only to discover that a gardener had left the door to the garage open and a neighborhood dog had enjoyed the feast. For Thanksgiving, they ate in a restaurant, then drove around the neighborhood looking for a dog with heartburn.[229]

War

• Michael, the son of children's author Walter Dean Myers, served in the Persian Gulf War and came back to the United States safe and sound. About the experience of having a child serve as a soldier in a war, Mr. Myers says, "You hear this story about a woman waking up in the middle of the night in fear, and later she learns that her husband was killed at that exact moment. Well, that's a bunch of crap. The truth is, you wake up every night in fear. It was a very scary time." (Mr. Myers' younger brother died in Vietnam.)[230]

• One of Emma Washa's sons had an unenviable job during World War II. He worked in a hospital ward, and the wounded soldiers sometimes went crazy with pain and suffering. His job was to kneel on them to keep them from getting out of bed and hurting themselves. Later, this son died from a brain tumor. According to Ms. Washa, the brain tumor was caused by the insanity of war.[231]

Weddings

• In the first half of the 20th century, Edwin Porter was a preacher in Texas, where he performed many weddings. In those days, etiquette books said that $3 was the proper amount to pay the preacher for performing the wedding, but when asked what he was owed Rev. Porter simply answered, "Just pay me whatever you think your wife is worth." One new husband dug a quarter out of his pocket and asked if Rev. Porter had change! But another new husband dug into his pockets and hauled out bills, quarters, and other change, then he handed all his money to Rev. Porter without counting it, saying, "My wife is worth all I've got." (Because the marriage fees varied so widely, Rev. Porter's children made a game out of guessing the amount the groom would pay their father.)[232]

• In a Haverhill, Massachusetts, cemetery are several funeral stones dedicated to the wives of Captain Nathaniel Thurston. His final wife, who outlived him, is not there. During the good captain's final trip to the cemetery from Lansinburgh, New York, she rode beside his coffin in the undertaker's wagon while the undertaker and his son rode up front. On the way back home from the cemetery, she rode beside the undertaker up front while his son rode in back. When she and the undertaker returned back home to Lansinburgh, New York, they got married.[233]

• Aung San Suu Kyi of Burma fell in love with British citizen Michael Aris. In 1971, when he was working as a tutor in Bhutan for the royal family and she was working in New York City, she sent him 187 letters. They married even though Suu Kyi came from a prominent Burmese family and the Burmese people often are against intermarriage with foreigners. In fact, Chit Myaing, former Burmese ambassador to Great Britain, said, "The Burmese people would not like [Suu Kyi] marrying a foreigner. I knew that if I attended the wedding, I would be fired that day."[234]

• Frank Benson was the manager of a traveling Shakespearean troupe and a man who enjoyed sports. Once, he heard a rumor that one of his actors, Harold Large, was expected to ask a certain woman to marry him. Mr. Benson asked his wife, Constance, if she thought the woman would accept the marriage proposal. She replied, "I don't know. He hasn't made his fortune yet." This shocked Mr. Benson: "Good Heavens! I don't know what she wants — the fellow is one of the finest half-backs in England!"[235]

• One of Dini von Mueffling's best friends was Alison Gertz, who had contracted HIV, which developed into AIDS. Dini met a man, they fell in love, he asked her to marry him, and she accepted. However, Dini was worried about what Alison would say when she told her. She needn't have worried. After learning that the man, Richard, had asked Dini to marry him after knowing her for only three months, Alison asked, "What took him so long?"[236]

• Rabbi Shlomo Carlebach once wrote the wedding invitation for two of his friends, promising them, "It'll be the holiest wedding invitation in the world!" The invitation read, "The whole world is invited to the wedding of Ne'eman Rosen and Malka Gorman." The invitations were given out all through the Haight-Ashbury district, and attending the wedding were many people whom Mr. Rosen and Ms. Gorman didn't know.[237]

• In the late 1890s and early 1900s, educated women were rare. For example, Ernestine Carey was educated in college at a time when few women were and those few were looked at somewhat strangely. When she married Frank B. Gilbreth, Jr., a newspaper reported, "Although a graduate of the University of California, the bride is nonetheless an extremely attractive young woman."[238]

• A woman walked into a fabric shop and asked for a fabric that would rustle when she walked. The proprietor found a suitable fabric for her, then out of curiosity asked what she wanted it for. The woman replied, "I am getting married to a blind man, and I want to make a wedding dress that rustles when I walk down the aisle so my fiancé will know when I've arrived at the altar."[239]

• Sonja Ely's five-year-old granddaughter was holding a wedding for two of her dolls. At one point, she spoke for the groom, saying to the minister, "Now you can read us our rights." Speaking for the minister, she then said, "You have the right to remain silent, anything you say can be held against you, you have the right to have an attorney present. You may kiss the bride."[240]

• In 1982, figure skater Dorothy Hamill married Dean Paul Martin, the son of entertainer Dean Martin. President Ronald Reagan was one of her neighbors at the time, but she didn't invite him to the wedding because she feared that the presence of the Secret Service guards would interfere with the wedding and with the enjoyment of the guests.[241]

• Tom Cahill used to be the coach of the Army football team. He played his college football at Niagara, where he was once caught sneaking into bed at 3 a.m. His punishment for breaking training was to copy the text of an entire book. He chose *Selecting a Mate in Marriage* and copied it from 9 p.m. to 7 a.m.[242]

• Richard Vaux, a Quaker, was secretary to a legation that appeared at the English court. He fit in well at court and wrote home that he had danced with Princess Victoria (who later became Queen of England). His mother read the letter, then remarked, "I do hope Richard won't marry out of meeting."[243]

• A Harvard football star was getting married. As he knelt before the bishop, the guests started laughing. The ushers — all of whom were football fans — had printed on the sole of his left shoe "TO HELL" and on the sole of his right shoe "WITH YALE."[244]

Widows

• Dipa Ma started studying meditation after she fell into a deep depression after the sudden death of her husband, which followed the deaths of two of her children. She asked herself, "What can I take with me when I die?" Looking around, she saw many material possessions and her daughter, but nothing she could take with her when she died. She then thought, "Let me go to the meditation center. Maybe I can find something there I can take with me when I die." In meditation, she found peace.[245]

• Women of the west gained respect from men of the west. After a widow travelling west succeeded through sheer determination in getting her children alive through Death Valley, the men traveling with her agreed that "she was the best man of the party."[246]

Work

• Aryeh Labe, aka Archie Lionel, was the youngest brother of the mother of Al Capp, creator of the comic strip *Li'l Abner*. As a young man, he didn't know whether to become a rabbi or a dancer. One day, Aryeh and two friends visited his sister's family. After eating, the two friends put on a dance demonstration for the family. They were magnificent, and Al's mother asked her brother, "Archie, *kind*, can you dance that way?" Archie replied, "Never in a million years." Hearing that, she advised her brother, "Then, Archie, *tierer*, become a rabbi." He did. (By the way, the friends really were magnificent dancers. Their names were Arthur and Katherine Murray.)[247]

• Pulitzer Prize-winning reporter Meyer Berger was very poor when he was growing up. As a child, he and two brothers — one older, one younger — got up early to sell newspapers in diners. After the first batch of newspapers was sold, the youngest brother quit working; after the second batch was sold, Meyer quit working; finally, after all the newspapers were sold, the oldest brother quit working. As an adult, Meyer would sometimes arrive at work carrying a dozen copies of the same newspaper — he never said no to a newsboy.[248]

• While appearing as a lecturer across the country, Will Rogers included a comic bit in which he and his nephew moved a piano across the stage. The nephew did the hard work of moving the piano, while Will "helped" by moving the piano stool. One night, an accident occurred on stage. The piano collapsed, the audience laughed, and Will said later, "I wish it would happen every night."[249]

• Eugene Field wanted a raise while he was working for the *Chicago Daily News*. So one day he and his four small children dressed in rags and went inside the editor's office, where the children begged, "Please, sir, won't you raise our father's wages?"[250]

Appendix A: Bibliography

Aaseng, Rolf E. *Anyone Can Teach (they said)*. Minneapolis, MN: Augsburg Publishing House, 1965.

Adler, Bill. *The Letterman Wit: His Life and Humor*. New York: Carroll & Graf Publishers, Inc., 1994.

Adler, Bill, and Bruce Cassiday. *The World of Jay Leno: His Humor and His Life*. New York: Carol Publishing Group, 1992.

Alda, Frances. *Men, Women, and Tenors*. Boston, MA: Houghton Mifflin Company, 1937.

Alley, Ken. *Awkward Christian Soldiers*. Wheaton, IL: Harold Shaw Publishers, 1998.

Arden, Eve. *Three Phases of Eve: An Autobiography*. New York: St. Martin's Press, 1985.

Barnhouse, Donald Grey. *Let Me Illustrate: Stories, Anecdotes, Illustrations*. Westwood, NJ: Fleming H. Revell Company, 1967.

Benson, Constance. *Mainly Players: Bensonian Memories*. London: Thornton Butterworth, Ltd., 1926.

Berger, Phil. *The Last Laugh: The World of the Stand-Up Comics*. New York: William Morris and Co., Inc., 1975.

Bernard, André. *Now All We Need is a Title: Famous Book Titles and How They Got That Way*. New York: W.W. Norton & Company, 1995.

Blumberg, Arthur, and Phyllis Blumberg. *The Unwritten Curriculum: Things Learned But Not Taught in Schools*. Thousand Oaks, CA: Corwin Press, Inc., 1994.

Bombeck, Erma. *I Want to Grow Hair, I Want to Grow Up, I Want to Go to Boise*. New York: Harper and Row, Publishers, 1989.

Bono, Chastity. *Family Outing*. With Billie Fitzpatrick. Boston, MA: Little, Brown and Company, 1998.

Bourke, Dale Hanson. *Everyday Miracles: Holy Moments in a Mother's Day*. Dallas, TX: Word Publishing, 1989.

Boxer, Tim. *The Jewish Celebrity Hall of Fame*. New York: Shapolsky Publishers, 1987.

Brady, Logan Munger. *Amusing Anecdotes: Humorous Stories With a Moral*. Ann Arbor, MI: Ann Arbor Book Company, 1993.

Brennan, Christine. *Inside Edge: A Revealing Journey into the Secret World of Figure Skating*. New York: Scribner, 1996.

Brown, Cordell. *I am What I am by the Grace of God*. Warsaw, OH: Echoing Hills Village Foundation, 1996.

Brown, Joe E. *Laughter is a Wonderful Thing*. As told to Ralph Hancock. New York: A.S. Barnes and Co., 1956.

Bryan III, J. *Merry Gentlemen (and One Lady)*. New York: Atheneum, 1985.

Burchard, S.H. *Dorothy Hamill*. New York: Harcourt Brace Jovanovich, 1978.

Burke, John. *Rogue's Progress: The Fabulous Adventures of Wilson Mizner*. New York: G.P. Putnam's Sons, 1975.

Campbell, Archie. *Archie Campbell: An Autobiography*. With Ben Bryd. Memphis, TN: Memphis State University Press, 1981.

Cantor, Eddie. *The Way I See It*. Englewood Cliffs, NJ: 1959.

Caplin, Elliott. *Al Capp Remembered*. Bowling Green, OH: Bowling Green State University Popular Press, 1994.

Carpenter, Angelica Shirley, and Jean Shirley. *Frances Hodgson Burnett: Beyond the Secret Garden*. Minneapolis, MN: Lerner Publications Company, 1990.

Carter, Judy. *The Homo Handbook*. New York: Fireside Books, 1996.

Charles, Helen White, collector and editor. *Quaker Chuckles and Other True Stories About Friends*. Oxford, OH: H.W. Charles, 1961.

Châtaigneau, Gérard, and Steve Milton. *Figure Skating Now: Olympic and World Stars*. Willowdale, Ontario, Canada: Firefly Books, 2001.

Chenevière, Alain. *Maud in France*. Minneapolis, MN: Lerner Publications Company, 1996.

Clemens, Cyril, editor. *Mark Twain Anecdotes*. Webster Groves, MO: Mark Twain Society, 1929.

Clinton, Kate. *Don't Get Me Started*. New York: Ballantine Books, 1998.

Clower, Jerry. *Life Everlaughter: The Heart and Humor of Jerry Clower*. Nashville, TN: Rutledge Hill Press, 1987.

Conner, Bart. *Winning the Gold*. With Coach Paul Ziert. New York: Warner Books, Inc., 1985.

David, Jay. *The Life and Humor of Robin Williams*. New York: William Morrow and Company, Inc., 1999.

DeCaro, Frank. *A Boy Named Phyllis*. New York: Viking, 1996.

Dole, Bob. *Great Political Wit*. New York: Doubleday, 1998.

Dosick, Wayne. *Golden Rules: The Ten Ethical Rules Parents Need to Teach Their Children*. San Francisco, CA: HarperSanFrancisco, 1995.

Drennan, Robert E., editor. *The Algonquin Wits*. New York: The Citadel Press, 1968.

Edwards, Susan. *Erma Bombeck: A Life in Humor*. New York: Avon Books, 1997.

Epstein, Lawrence J. *A Treasury of Jewish Anecdotes*. Northvale, NJ: Jason Aronson, Inc., 1989.

Ewen, David, complier. *Listen to the Mocking Words*. New York: Arco Publishing Co., 1945.

Fadiman, James, and Robert Frager. *Essential Sufism*. San Francisco, CA: HarperSanFrancisco, 1997.

Farrell, Suzanne. *Holding On to the Air*. New York: Summit Books, 1990.

Feinberg, Morris "Moe." *Larry: The Stooge in the Middle*. With G.P. Skratz. San Francisco, CA: Last Gasp of San Francisco, 1984.

Ford, Carin T. *Legends of American Dance and Choreography*. Berkeley Heights, NJ: Enslow Publications, Inc., 2000.

Ford, Michael Thomas. *The Voices of AIDS: Twelve Unforgettable People Talk About How AIDS has Changed Their Lives*. New York: Morrow Junior Books, 1995.

Fox, Grace. *Everyday Etiquette*. Garden City, New York: Doubleday Direct, Inc., 1996.

Frank, Rusty E. *Tap! The Greatest Tap Dance Stars and Their Stories, 1900-1955*. New York: William Morrow and Company, Inc., 1990.

Franks, A.H., editor. *Pavlova: A Collection of Memoirs*. New York: Da Capo Press, Inc., 1956.

Fuller, Gerald. *Stories for All Seasons*. Mystic, CT: Twenty-Third Publications, 1996.

Gallo, Hank. *Comedy Explosion: A New Generation*. Photographs by Ed Edahl. New York: Thunder's Mouth Press, 1991.

Garagiola, Joe. *It's Anybody's Ballgame*. New York: Jove Books, 1988.

Gershick, Zsa Zsa. *Gay Old Girls*. Los Angeles, CA: Alyson Books, 1998.

Gilbreth, Jr., Frank B. and Ernestine Gilbreth Carey. *Cheaper by the Dozen*. New York: Thomas Y. Crowell Company, 1948.

Gleasner, Diana C. *Track and Field*. New York: Harvey House, Publishers, 1977.

Gonzales, Doreen. *Diego Rivera: His Art, His Life*. Berkeley Heights, NJ: Enslow Publications, Inc., 1996.

Gordeeva, Ekaterina. *My Sergei: A Love Story*. With E.M. Swift. New York: Warner Books, Inc., 1996.

Greenberg, Keith Elliot. *Zack's Story*. Minneapolis, MN: Lerner Publications Company, 1996.

Grenfell, Joyce. *Joyce Grenfell Requests the Pleasure*. London: Macdonald Futura Publishers Ltd., 1976.

Guernsey, JoAnn Bren. *Tipper Gore: Voice for the Voiceless*. Minneapolis, MN: Lerner Publications Company, 1994.

Hall, Marilyn, and Rabbi Jerome Cutler. *The Celebrity Kosher Cookbook*. Los Angeles, CA: J.P. Tarcher, Inc., 1975.

Henry, Lewis C. *Humorous Anecdotes About Famous People*. Garden City, NY: Halcyon House, 1948.

Hill, Christine M. *Ten Terrific Authors for Teens*. Berkeley Heights, NJ: Enslow Publications, Inc., 2000.

Himelstein, Shmuel. *A Touch of Wisdom, A Touch of Wit*. Brooklyn, NY: Mesorah Publications, Limited, 1991.

Himelstein, Shmuel. *Words of Wisdom, Words of Wit*. Brooklyn, NY: Mesorah Publications, Ltd., 1993.

Howard, Megan. *Madeleine Albright*. Minneapolis, MN: Lerner Publications Company, 1999.

Jacobs, Linda. *Mary Decker: Speed Records and Spaghetti*. St. Paul, MN: EMI Corporation, 1975.

Jordan, Denise M. *Walter Dean Myers: Writer for Real Teens*. Berkeley Heights, NJ: Enslow Publications, Inc., 1999.

Josephson, Judith Pinkerton. *Nikki Giovanni: Poet of the People*. Berkeley Heights, NJ: Enslow Publications, Inc., 2000.

Kandel, Bethany. *Trevor's Story*. Minneapolis, MN: Lerner Publications Company, 1997.

Kanner, Bernice. *The 100 Best TV Commercials ... and Why They Worked*. New York: Times Books, 1999.

Karolyi, Bela, and Nancy Ann Richardson. *Feel No Fear: The Power, Passion, and Politics of a Life in Gymnastics*. New York: Hyperion, 1994.

Kistler, Darci. *Ballerina: My Story*. With Alicia Kistler. New York: Pocket Books, Inc., 1993.

Klinger, Kurt, collector. *A Pope Laughs: Stories of John XXIII*. Translated by Sally McDevitt Cunneen. New York: Holt, Rinehart and Winston, 1964.

Kramer, Barbara. *John Glenn: A Space Biography*. Springfield, NJ: Enslow Publications, Inc., 1998.

Laffey, Bruce. *Beatrice Lillie: The Funniest Woman in the World*. New York: Wynwood Press, 1989.

Laskas, Jeanne Marie. *We Remember: Women Born at the Turn of the Century Tell the Stories of Their Lives*. Photographs by Lynn Johnson. New York: William Morrow and Company, 1999.

Lewis, Mildred and Milton. *Famous Modern Newspaper Writers*. New York: Dodd, Mead & Company, 1962.

Linkletter, Art. *I Didn't Do It Alone: The Autobiography of Art Linkletter*. Ottawa, IL: Caroline House Publishers, Inc., 1980.

Linkletter, Art. *Oops! Or, Life's Awful Moments*. Garden City, NY: Doubleday & Company, Inc., 1967.

Lipinski, Tara, and Emily Costello. *Tara Lipinski: Triumph on Ice*. New York: Bantam Books, 1997.

Madison, Bob. *American Horror Writers*. Berkeley Heights, NJ: Enslow Publications, Inc., 2001.

Malone, Mary. *Will Rogers: Cowboy Philosopher*. Springfield, NJ: Enslow Publications, Inc., 1996.

Mandelbaum, Yitta Halberstam. *Holy Brother: Inspiring Stories and Enchanted Tales About Rabbi Shlomo Carlebach*. Northvale, NJ: Jason Aronson, Inc., 1997.

Marx, Arthur. *Life With Groucho*. New York: Simon and Schuster, 1954.

Maverick, Jr., Maury. *Texas Iconoclast*. Edited by Allan O. Kownslar. Fort Worth, TX: Texas Christian University Press, 1997.

McCann, Sean, compiler. *The Wit of the Irish*. Nashville, TN: Aurora Publishers, Ltd., 1970.

Michaels, Louis. *The Humor and Warmth of Pope John XXIII: His Anecdotes and Legends*. New York: Pocket Books, Inc., 1965.

Miller, Brandon Marie. *Buffalo Gals: Women of the Old West*. Minneapolis, MN: Lerner Publications Company, 1995.

Miller, Claudia. *Shannon Miller: My Child, My Hero*. Norman, OK: University of Oklahoma Press, 1999.

Mindess, Harvey. *The Chosen People? A Testament, Both Old and New, to the Therapeutic Power of Jewish Wit and Humor*. Los Angeles, CA: Nash Publishing Corporation, 1972.

Mockridge, Norton. *A Funny Thing Happened* .... Greenwich, CT: Fawcett Publications, Inc., 1966.

Morgan, Henry. *Here's Morgan!* New York: Barricade Books, Inc., 1994.

Morley, Robert. *Around the World in Eighty-One Years*. London: Hodder & Stoughton, 1990.

Mostel, Kate, and Madeline Gilford. *170 Years of Show Business*. With Jack Gilford and Zero Mostel. New York: Random House, 1978.

Northrup, Mary. *American Computer Pioneers*. Springfield, NJ: Enslow Publications, Inc., 1998.

Pike, Robert E. *Granite Laughter and Marble Tears*. Brattleboro, VT: Stephen Daye Press, 1938.

Poley, Irvin C., and Ruth Verlenden Poley. *Friendly Anecdotes*. New York: Harper & Brothers, Publishers, 1950.

Porter, Alyene. *Papa was a Preacher*. New York: Abingdon Press, 1944.

Roessel, Monty. *Kinaaldá: A Navajo Girl Grows Up*. Minneapolis, MN: Lerner Publications Company, 1993.

Rogers, Fred. *Dear Mister Rogers, Does It Ever Rain in Your Neighborhood? Letters to Mister Rogers*. New York: Penguin Books, 1996.

Rogers, Fred. *You Are Special*. New York: Viking, 1994.

Rowell, Edward K., editor. *Humor for Preaching and Teaching*. Grand Rapids, MI: Baker Books, 1996.

Salzberg, Sharon. *A Heart as Wide as the World: Stories on the Path to Lovingkindness*. Boston, MA: Shambhala Publications, Inc., 1997.

Samra, Cal and Rose, editors. *More Holy Hilarity*. Colorado Springs, CO: WaterBrook Press, 1999.

Sanford, William R., and Carl R. Green. *Dorothy Hamill*. New York: Crestwood House, 1993.

Schafer, Kermit. *All Time Great Bloopers*. New York: Avenel Books, 1973.

Schafer, Kermit. *Best of Bloopers*. New York: Avenel Books, 1973.

Schraff, Anne. *Ralph Bunche: Winner of the Nobel Peace Prize*. Berkeley Heights, NJ: Enslow Publications, Inc., 1999.

Schulman, Arlene. *Carmine's Story*. Minneapolis, MN: Lerner Publications Company, 1997.

Sessions, William H., collector. *Laughter in Quaker Grey*. York, England: William Sessions Limited, 1966.

Sessions, William H., collector. *More Quaker Laughter*. York, England: William Sessions Limited, 1974.

Shawn, Ted. *One Thousand and One Night Stands*. With Gray Poole. New York: Da Capo Press, Inc., 1979.

Slezak, Leo. *Song of Motley*. New York: Arno Press, 1977.

Smith, Bob. *Openly Bob*. New York: William Morrow and Company, Inc., 1997.

Smith, H. Allen. *The Compleat Practical Joker*. Garden City, NY: Doubleday and Company, Inc., 1953.

Stewart, Whitney. *Aung San Suu Kyi: Fearless Voice of Burma*. Minneapolis, MN: Lerner Publications Company, 1997.

Strug, Kerri. *Landing on My Feet: A Diary of Dreams*. With John P. Lopez. Kansas City, MO: Andrews McMeel Publishing, 1997.

Taylor, Robert Lewis. *W.C. Fields: His Follies and Fortunes*. Garden City, NY: Doubleday and Company, Inc., 1949.

Telushkin, Rabbi Joseph. *Jewish Wisdom: Ethical, Spiritual, and Historical Lessons from the Great Works and Thinkers*. New York: William Morrow and Company, Inc., 1994.

Tobias, Andrew. *The Best Little Boy in the World Grows Up*. New York: Random House, 1998.

Ward, Gene and Dick Hyman, collectors. *Football Wit and Humor*. New York: Grosset & Dunlap, Publishers, 1970.

Watson, Richard. *The Philosopher's Diet: How to Lose Weight and Change the World*. Boston, MA: The Atlantic Monthly Press, 1985.

Williams, Kenneth. *Acid Drops*. London: J.M. Dent & Sons, Ltd., 1980.

Willson, Meredith. *And There I Stood With My Piccolo*. Westport, CT: Greenwood Press, Publishers, 1948.

Woughter, William. *All Preachers of Our God & King*. Wheaton, IL: Harold Shaw Publishers, 1997.

Youngman, Henny. *Take My Life, Please!* With Neal Karlen. New York: William Morris and Company, Inc., 1991.

Appendix B: About the Author

It was a dark and stormy night. Suddenly a cry rang out, and on a hot summer night in 1954, Josephine, wife of Carl Bruce, gave birth to a boy — me. Unfortunately, this young married couple allowed Reuben Saturday, Josephine's brother, to name their first-born. Reuben, aka "The Joker," decided that Bruce was a nice name, so he decided to name me Bruce Bruce. I have gone by my middle name — David — ever since.

Being named Bruce David Bruce hasn't been all bad. Bank tellers remember me very quickly, so I don't often have to show an ID. It can be fun in charades, also. When I was a counselor as a teenager at Camp Echoing Hills in Warsaw, Ohio, a fellow counselor gave the signs for "sounds like" and "two words," then she pointed to a bruise on her leg twice. Bruise Bruise? Oh yeah, Bruce Bruce is the answer!

Uncle Reuben, by the way, is the guy who gave me a haircut when I was in kindergarten. He cut my hair short and shaved a small bald spot on the back of my head. My mother wouldn't let me go to school until the bald spot grew out again.

Of all my brothers and sisters (six in all), I am the only transplant to Athens, Ohio. I was born in Newark, Ohio, and have lived all around Southeastern Ohio. However, I moved to Athens to go to Ohio University and have never left.

At Ohio U, I never could make up my mind whether to major in English or Philosophy, so I got a bachelor's degree with a double major in both areas, then I added a Master of Arts degree in English and a Master of Arts degree in Philosophy. Yes, I have my MAMA degree.

Currently, and for a long time to come (I eat fruits and veggies), I am spending my retirement writing books such as *Nadia Comaneci: Perfect 10*, *The Funniest People in Comedy*, *Homer's* Iliad: *A Retelling in Prose*, and *William Shakespeare's* Hamlet: *A Retelling in Prose*.

If all goes well, I will publish one or two books a year for the rest of my life. (On the other hand, a good way to make God laugh is to tell Her your plans.)

By the way, my sister Brenda Kennedy writes romances such as *A New Beginning* and *Shattered Dreams*.

Appendix C: Some Books by David Bruce

Anecdote Collections

250 Anecdotes About Opera
250 Anecdotes About Religion
250 Anecdotes About Religion: Volume 2
250 Music Anecdotes
Be a Work of Art: 250 Anecdotes and Stories
Boredom is Anti-Life: 250 Anecdotes and Stories
The Coolest People in Art: 250 Anecdotes
The Coolest People in the Arts: 250 Anecdotes
The Coolest People in Books: 250 Anecdotes
The Coolest People in Comedy: 250 Anecdotes
Create, Then Take a Break: 250 Anecdotes
Don't Fear the Reaper: 250 Anecdotes
The Funniest People in Art: 250 Anecdotes
The Funniest People in Books: 250 Anecdotes
The Funniest People in Books, Volume 2: 250 Anecdotes
The Funniest People in Books, Volume 3: 250 Anecdotes
The Funniest People in Comedy: 250 Anecdotes
The Funniest People in Dance: 250 Anecdotes
The Funniest People in Families: 250 Anecdotes
The Funniest People in Families, Volume 2: 250 Anecdotes
The Funniest People in Families, Volume 3: 250 Anecdotes
The Funniest People in Families, Volume 4: 250 Anecdotes
The Funniest People in Families, Volume 5: 250 Anecdotes
The Funniest People in Families, Volume 6: 250 Anecdotes
The Funniest People in Movies: 250 Anecdotes
The Funniest People in Music: 250 Anecdotes
The Funniest People in Music, Volume 2: 250 Anecdotes
The Funniest People in Music, Volume 3: 250 Anecdotes
The Funniest People in Neighborhoods: 250 Anecdotes
The Funniest People in Relationships: 250 Anecdotes
The Funniest People in Sports: 250 Anecdotes
The Funniest People in Sports, Volume 2: 250 Anecdotes
The Funniest People in Television and Radio: 250 Anecdotes

The Funniest People in Theater: 250 Anecdotes
The Funniest People Who Live Life: 250 Anecdotes
The Funniest People Who Live Life, Volume 2: 250 Anecdotes
The Kindest People Who Do Good Deeds, Volume 1: 250 Anecdotes
The Kindest People Who Do Good Deeds, Volume 2: 250 Anecdotes
Maximum Cool: 250 Anecdotes
The Most Interesting People in Movies: 250 Anecdotes
The Most Interesting People in Politics and History: 250 Anecdotes
The Most Interesting People in Politics and History, Volume 2: 250 Anecdotes
The Most Interesting People in Politics and History, Volume 3: 250 Anecdotes
The Most Interesting People in Religion: 250 Anecdotes
The Most Interesting People in Sports: 250 Anecdotes
The Most Interesting People Who Live Life: 250 Anecdotes
The Most Interesting People Who Live Life, Volume 2: 250 Anecdotes
Reality is Fabulous: 250 Anecdotes and Stories
Resist Psychic Death: 250 Anecdotes
Seize the Day: 250 Anecdotes and Stories

Appendix C: Some Books by David Bruce

Anecdote Collections

250 Anecdotes About Opera

250 Anecdotes About Religion

250 Anecdotes About Religion: Volume 2

250 Music Anecdotes

Be a Work of Art: 250 Anecdotes and Stories

Boredom is Anti-Life: 250 Anecdotes and Stories

The Coolest People in Art: 250 Anecdotes

The Coolest People in the Arts: 250 Anecdotes

The Coolest People in Books: 250 Anecdotes

The Coolest People in Comedy: 250 Anecdotes

Create, Then Take a Break: 250 Anecdotes

Don't Fear the Reaper: 250 Anecdotes

The Funniest People in Art: 250 Anecdotes

The Funniest People in Books: 250 Anecdotes

The Funniest People in Books, Volume 2: 250 Anecdotes

The Funniest People in Books, Volume 3: 250 Anecdotes

The Funniest People in Comedy: 250 Anecdotes

The Funniest People in Dance: 250 Anecdotes

The Funniest People in Families: 250 Anecdotes

The Funniest People in Families, Volume 2: 250 Anecdotes

The Funniest People in Families, Volume 3: 250 Anecdotes

The Funniest People in Families, Volume 4: 250 Anecdotes

The Funniest People in Families, Volume 5: 250 Anecdotes

The Funniest People in Families, Volume 6: 250 Anecdotes

The Funniest People in Movies: 250 Anecdotes

The Funniest People in Music: 250 Anecdotes

The Funniest People in Music, Volume 2: 250 Anecdotes

The Funniest People in Music, Volume 3: 250 Anecdotes

The Funniest People in Neighborhoods: 250 Anecdotes

The Funniest People in Relationships: 250 Anecdotes

The Funniest People in Sports: 250 Anecdotes

The Funniest People in Sports, Volume 2: 250 Anecdotes

The Funniest People in Television and Radio: 250 Anecdotes

The Funniest People in Theater: 250 Anecdotes
The Funniest People Who Live Life: 250 Anecdotes
The Funniest People Who Live Life, Volume 2: 250 Anecdotes
The Kindest People Who Do Good Deeds, Volume 1: 250 Anecdotes
The Kindest People Who Do Good Deeds, Volume 2: 250 Anecdotes
Maximum Cool: 250 Anecdotes
The Most Interesting People in Movies: 250 Anecdotes
The Most Interesting People in Politics and History: 250 Anecdotes
The Most Interesting People in Politics and History, Volume 2: 250 Anecdotes
The Most Interesting People in Politics and History, Volume 3: 250 Anecdotes
The Most Interesting People in Religion: 250 Anecdotes
The Most Interesting People in Sports: 250 Anecdotes
The Most Interesting People Who Live Life: 250 Anecdotes
The Most Interesting People Who Live Life, Volume 2: 250 Anecdotes
Reality is Fabulous: 250 Anecdotes and Stories
Resist Psychic Death: 250 Anecdotes
Seize the Day: 250 Anecdotes and Stories

[1] Source: Bill Adler and Bruce Cassiday, *The World of Jay Leno: His Humor and His Life*, p. 109.

[2] Source: Helen White Charles, collector and editor, *Quaker Chuckles*, p. 25.

[3] Source: Darci Kistler, *Ballerina: My Story*, p. 16.

[4] Source: Kermit Schafer, *Best of Bloopers*, p. 42.

[5] Source: Megan Howard, *Madeleine Albright*, p. 35.

[6] Source: Bill Adler and Bruce Cassiday, *The World of Jay Leno: His Humor and His Life*, p. 6.

[7] Source: Susan Edwards, *Erma Bombeck*, p. 160.

[8] Source: Henry Morgan, *Here's Morgan!*, pp. 64-65.

[9] Source: Art Linkletter, *I Didn't Do It Alone*, p. 88.

[10] Source: Eddie Cantor, *The Way I See It*, p. 192.

[11] Source: Eve Arden, *Three Phases of Eve*, p. 97.

[12] Source: Arlene Schulman, *Carmine's Story*, pp. 5, 31, 33.

[13] Source: Henry Morgan, *Here's Morgan!*, p. 295.

[14] Source: J. Bryan III, *Merry Gentlemen (and One Lady)*, p. 83.

[15] Source: Arthur Blumberg and Phyllis Blumberg, *The Unwritten Curriculum*, pp. 108-109.

[16] Source: Denise M. Jordan, *Walter Dean Myers: Writer for Real Teens*, pp. 82, 89-90.

[17] Source: Christine M. Hill, *Ten Terrific Authors for Teens*, p. 10.

[18] Source: James Fadiman and Robert Frager, *Essential Sufism*, p. 186.

[19] Source: Cordell Brown, *I am What I am by the Grace of God*, p. 33.

[20] Source: John Burke, *Rogue's Progress: The Fabulous Adventures of Wilson Mizner*, p. 245.

[21] Source: Tim Boxer, *The Jewish Celebrity Hall of Fame*, p. 127.

[22] Source: Alain Chenevière, *Maud in France*, pp. 4-7.

[23] Source: Bela Karolyi and Nancy Ann Richardson, *Feel No Fear*, pp. 127-128.

[24] Source: Leo Slezak, *Song of Motley*, pp. 127-128.

[25] Source: Morris "Moe" Feinberg, *Larry: The Stooge in the Middle*, pp. 142-143.

[26] Source: Bob Madison, *American Horror Writers*, pp. 73, 75-76.

[27] Source: Claudia Miller, *Shannon Miller: My Child, My Hero*, p. 34.

[28] Source: Fred Rogers, *You Are Special*, p. 40.

[29] Source: Frank B. Gilbreth, Jr., and Ernestine Gilbreth Carey, *Cheaper by the Dozen*, p. 22.

[30] Source: Diana C. Gleasner, *Track and Field*, p. 44.

[31] Source: Dale Hanson Bourke, *Everyday Miracles*, pp. 55-56.

[32] Source: Robert Lewis Taylor, *W.C. Fields: His Follies and Fortunes*, p. 23.

[33] Source: Barbara Kramer, *John Glenn: A Space Biography*, p. 12.

[34] Source: Kenneth Williams, *Acid Drops*, p. 47.

[35] Source: Angelica Shirley Carpenter and Jean Shirley, *Frances Hodgson Burnett: Beyond the Secret Garden*, p. 46.

[36] Source: Shmuel Himelstein, *A Touch of Wisdom, A Touch of Wit*, p. 235.

[37] Source: Arthur Marx, *Life With Groucho*, p. 296.

[38] Source: Joe E. Brown, *Laughter is a Wonderful Thing*, p. 214.

[39] Source: Sharon Salzberg, *A Heart as Wide as the World*, pp. 102-103.

[40] Source: Rolf E. Aaseng, *Anyone Can Teach (they said)*, p. 63.

[41] Source: Ken Alley, *Awkward Christian Soldiers*, pp. 49-50.

[42] Source: William Woughter, *All Preachers of Our God & King*, p. 10.

[43] Source: Erma Bombeck, *I Want to Grow Hair, I Want to Grow Up, I Want to Go to Boise*, p. 116.

[44] Source: Joyce Grenfell, *Joyce Grenfell Requests the Pleasure*, p. 12.

[45] Source: Kermit Schafer, *All Time Great Bloopers*, p. 20.

[46] Source: David Ewen, *Listen to the Mocking Words*, p. 40.

[47] Source: Doreen Gonzales, *Diego Rivera: His Art, His Life*, p. 64.

[48] Source: Jerry Clower, *Life Everlaughter*, p. 66.

[49] Source: A.H. Franks, editor, *Pavlova: A Collection of Memoirs*, p. 44.

[50] Source: Alyene Porter, *Papa Was a Preacher*, pp. 146-147.

[51] Source: Dale Hanson Bourke, *Everyday Miracles*, pp. 34-35.

[52] Source: Kurt Klinger, *A Pope Laughs*, pp. 20-21.

[53] Source: Judith Pinkerton Josephson, *Nikki Giovanni: Poet of the People*, p. 21.

[54] Source: Leo Slezak, *Song of Motley*, pp. 129-130.

[55] Source: Louis Michaels, *The Humor and Warmth of Pope John XXIII*, pp. 10-11.

[56] Source: William H. Sessions, collector, *More Quaker Laughter*, p. 31.

[57] Source: Kate Mostel and Madeline Gilford, *170 Years of Show Business*, pp. 77-78.

[58] Source: William Woughter, *All Preachers of Our God & King*, pp. 85-86.

[59] Source: Linda Jacobs, *Mary Decker: Speed Records and Spaghetti*, pp. 26, 28.

[60] Source: Judy Carter, *The Homo Handbook*, p. 177.

[61] Source: Rabbi Joseph Telushkin, *Jewish Wisdom*, pp. 175-176.

[62] Source: Bob Dole, *Great Political Wit*, p. 30.

[63] Source: Robert Morley, *Around the World in Eighty-One Years*, p. 46.

[64] Source: Cal and Rose Samra, *More Holy Hilarity*, pp. 145-146.

[65] Source: Elliott Caplin, *Al Capp Remembered*, pp. 19-20.

[66] Source: Bruce Laffey, *Beatrice Lillie*, p. 237.

[67] Source: Richard Watson, *The Philosopher's Diet*, p. 147.

[68] Source: Shmuel Himelstein, *Words of Wisdom, Words of Wit*, p. 166.

[69] Source: Grace Fox, *Everyday Etiquette*, p. 270.

[70] Source: Linda Jacobs, *Mary Decker: Speed Records and Spaghetti*, pp. 37-38.

[71] Source: Henny Youngman, *Take My Life, Please!*, p. 207.

[72] Source: Cal and Rose Samra, *More Holy Hilarity*, p. 185.

[73] Source: Anne Schraff, *Ralph Bunche: Winner of the Nobel Peace Prize*, pp. 17-18, 21, 115-116.

[74] Source: Bela Karolyi and Nancy Ann Richardson, *Feel No Fear*, p. 135.

[75] Source: Kurt Klinger, *A Pope Laughs*, p. 17.

[76] Source: Ken Alley, *Awkward Christian Soldiers*, pp. 86-87.

[77] Source: Wayne Dosick, *Golden Rules*, pp. 51-52.

[78] Source: Suzanne Farrell, *Holding On to the Air*, pp. 19, 35.

[79] Source: Arthur Blumberg and Phyllis Blumberg, *The Unwritten Curriculum*, pp. 15-17.

[80] Source: Logan Munger Brady, *Amusing Anecdotes*, p. 26.

[81] Source: William H. Sessions, collector, *Laughter in Quaker Grey*, p. 105.

[82] Source: Megan Howard, *Madeleine Albright*, pp. 38-39.

[83] Source: Phil Berger, *The Last Laugh*, pp. 238-239.

[84] Source: Carin T. Ford, *Legends of American Dance and Choreography*, p. 7.

[85] Source: Gérard Châtaigneau and Steve Milton, *Figure Skating Now: Olympic and World Stars*, p. 46.

[86] Source: Kerri Strug, *Landing on My Feet*, p. 5.

[87] Source: Claudia Miller, *Shannon Miller: My Child, My Hero*, p. 41.

[88] Source: Cordell Brown, *I am What I am by the Grace of God*, p. 169.

[89] Source: Bob Smith, *Openly Bob*, p. 3.

[90] Source: Rabbi Joseph Telushkin, *Jewish Wisdom*, p. 151.

[91] Source: Joe Garagiola, *It's Anybody's Ballgame*, pp. 225-226.

[92] Source: Meredith Willson, *And There I Stood With My Piccolo*, pp. 73-74.

[93] Source: Lawrence J. Epstein, *A Treasury of Jewish Anecdotes*, p. 22.

[94] Source: Kermit Schafer, *Best of Bloopers*, p. 92.

[95] Source: Hank Gallo, *Comedy Explosion: A New Generation*, p. 72.

[96] Source: Wayne Dosick, *Golden Rules*, pp. 80-81.

[97] Source: Gérard Châtaigneau and Steve Milton, *Figure Skating Now: Olympic and World Stars*, p. 115.

[98] Source: Whitney Stewart, *Aung San Suu Kyi: Fearless Voice of Burma*, pp. 31-32.

[99] Source: Marilyn Hall and Rabbi Jerome Cutler, *The Celebrity Kosher Cookbook*, p. 101.

[100] Source: Norton Mockridge, *A Funny Thing Happened ...*, p. 12.

[101] Source: Eddie Cantor, *The Way I See It*, p. 138.

[102] Source: Rolf E. Aaseng, *Anyone Can Teach (they said)*, pp. 93-94.

[103] Source: Brandon Marie Miller, *Buffalo Gals: Women of the Old West*, p. 14.

[104] Source: Helen White Charles, collector and editor, *Quaker Chuckles*, p. 58.

[105] Source: Andrew Tobias, *The Best Little Boy in the World Grows Up*, pp. 29-31.

[106] Source: Zsa Zsa Gershick, *Gay Old Girls*, p. 69.

[107] Source: Kate Clinton, *Don't Get Me Started*, p. 27.

[108] Source: Judy Carter, *The Homo Handbook*, p. 126.

[109] Source: Irvin C. Poley and Ruth Verlenden Poley, *Friendly Anecdotes*, pp. 118-119.

[110] Source: William R. Sanford and Carl R. Green, *Dorothy Hamill*, p. 14.

[111] Source: Christine M. Hill, *Ten Terrific Authors for Teens*, p. 94.

[112] Source: Ted Shawn, *One Thousand and One Night Stands*, pp. 44, 49-50.

[113] Source: Frances Alda, *Men, Women, and Tenors*, pp. 103-104.

[114] Source: Alain Chenevière, *Maud in France*, pp. 17, 20-21, 24.

[115] Source: Donald Grey Barnhouse, *Let Me Illustrate*, pp. 34-35.

[116] Source: Ekaterina Gordeeva, *My Sergei*, p. 22.

[117] Source: Meredith Willson, *And There I Stood With My Piccolo*, p. 75.

[118] Source: Fred Rogers, *You Are Special*, p. xii.

[119] Source: Maury Maverick, Jr., *Texas Iconoclast*, pp. 29-30.

[120] Source: Anne Schraff, *Ralph Bunche: Winner of the Nobel Peace Prize*, p. 22.

[121] Source: Frank DeCaro, *A Boy Named Phyllis*, p. 24.

[122] Source: Jerry Clower, *Life Everlaughter*, pp. 53-54.

[123] Source: David Ewen, *Listen to the Mocking Words*, pp. 77-78.

[124] Source: Bill Adler, *The Letterman Wit: His Life and Humor*, pp. 10-11.

[125] Source: Darci Kistler, *Ballerina: My Story*, pp. 19, 99.

[126] Source: Archie Campbell, *Archie Campbell: An Autobiography*, pp. 81-82.

[127] Source: Diana C. Gleasner, *Track and Field*, pp. 22-23.

[128] Source: Gerald Fuller, *Stories for All Seasons*, p. 41.

[129] Source: Art Linkletter, *Oops!*, pp. 67-68.

[130] Source: Constance Benson, *Mainly Players*, pp. 52-53.

[131] Source: Zsa Zsa Gershick, *Gay Old Girls*, p. 8.

[132] Source: Morris "Moe" Feinberg, *Larry: The Stooge in the Middle*, pp. 204, 206.

[133] Source: Sean McCann, compiler, *The Wit of the Irish*, p. 40.

[134] Source: Henny Youngman, *Take My Life, Please!*, p. 21.

[135] Source: Lawrence J. Epstein, *A Treasury of Jewish Anecdotes*, p. 251.

[136] Source: André Bernard, *Now All We Need is a Title*, p. 23.

[137] Source: Phil Berger, *The Last Laugh*, p. 122.

[138] Source: Lewis C. Henry, *Humorous Anecdotes About Famous People*, pp. 37-38.

[139] Source: André Bernard, *Now All We Need is a Title*, p. 76.

[140] Source: Bob Dole, *Great Political Wit*, pp. 75-76.

[141] Source: Robert E. Drennan, editor, *The Algonquin Wits*, p. 64.

[142] Source: Donald Grey Barnhouse, *Let Me Illustrate*, p. 36.

[143] Source: Robert Morley, *Around the World in Eighty-One Years*, p. 33.

[144] Source: Kenneth Williams, *Acid Drops*, p. 74.

[145] Source: Kermit Schafer, *All Time Great Bloopers*, p. 88.

[146] Source: Andrew Tobias, *The Best Little Boy in the World Grows Up*, pp. 13-14.

[147] Source: Ted Shawn, *One Thousand and One Night Stands*, p. 81.

[148] Source: Cyril Clemens, editor, *Mark Twain Anecdotes*, p. 20.

[149] Source: A.H. Franks, editor, *Pavlova: A Collection of Memoirs*, p. 58.

[150] Source: Hank Gallo, *Comedy Explosion: A New Generation*, p. 75.

[151] Source: Kate Mostel and Madeline Gilford, *170 Years of Show Business*, p. 127.

[152] Source: Fred Rogers, *Dear Mister Rogers, Does It Ever Rain in Your Neighborhood? Letters to Mister Rogers*, pp. 67-68.

[153] Source: Susan Edwards, *Erma Bombeck*, p. 182.

[154] Source: JoAnn Bren Guernsey, *Tipper Gore: Voice for the Voiceless*, pp. 39-40.

[155] Source: Arlene Schulman, *Carmine's Story*, pp. 8, 15.

[156] Source: Erma Bombeck, *I Want to Grow Hair, I Want to Grow Up, I Want to Go to Boise*, p. 92.

[157] Source: Cyril Clemens, editor, *Mark Twain Anecdotes*, p. 9.

[158] Source: Bernice Kanner, *The 100 Best TV Commercials*, p. 180.

[159] Source: Sean McCann, compiler, *The Wit of the Irish*, p. 71.

[160] Source: Bob Madison, *American Horror Writers*, p. 50.

[161] Source: Keith Elliot Greenberg, *Zack's Story*, p. 7.

[162] Source: John Burke, *Rogue's Progress: The Fabulous Adventures of Wilson Mizner*, pp. 94-95, 98-99.

[163] Source: Mildred and Milton Lewis, *Famous Modern Newspaper Writers*, pp. 32-33.

[164] Source: J. Bryan III, *Merry Gentlemen (and One Lady)*, p. 159.

[165] Source: H. Allen Smith, *The Compleat Practical Joker*, p. 256.

[166] Source: Mary Malone, *Will Rogers: Cowboy Philosopher*, p. 108.

[167] Source: Tim Boxer, *The Jewish Celebrity Hall of Fame*, pp. 47-48.

[168] Source: Michael Thomas Ford, *The Voices of AIDS*, pp. 84-85.

[169] Source: Bill Adler, *The Letterman Wit: His Life and Humor*, p. 98.

[170] Source: Bart Conner, *Winning the Gold*, p. 11.

[171] Source: Edward K. Rowell, editor, *Humor for Preaching and Teaching*, p. 80.

[172] Source: Carin T. Ford, *Legends of American Dance and Choreography*, p. 83.

[173] Source: Joyce Grenfell, *Joyce Grenfell Requests the Pleasure*, p. 245.

[174] Source: Robert Lewis Taylor, *W.C. Fields: His Follies and Fortunes*, p. 61.

[175] Source: Chastity Bono, *Family Outing*, pp. 92-93.

[176] Source: Monty Roessel, *Kinaaldá: A Navajo Girl Grows Up*, p. 22.

[177] Source: Eve Arden, *Three Phases of Eve*, p. 70.

[178] Source: Frank DeCaro, *A Boy Named Phyllis*, pp. 7-8.

[179] Source: Bob Smith, *Openly Bob*, p. 180.

[180] Source: Bart Conner, *Winning the Gold*, pp. 7-8.

[181] Source: Christine Brennan, *Inside Edge*, p. 168.

[182] Source: Frances Alda, *Men, Women, and Tenors*, p. 101.

[183] Source: Suzanne Farrell, *Holding On to the Air*, pp. 258-259.

[184] Source: Mary Northrup, *American Computer Pioneers*, p. 20.

[185] Source: Maury Maverick, Jr., *Texas Iconoclast*, pp. 233-234.

[186] Source: Shmuel Himelstein, *A Touch of Wisdom, A Touch of Wit*, p. 187.

[187] Source: Shmuel Himelstein, *Words of Wisdom, Words of Wit*, p. 36.

[188] Source: Tara Lipinski and Emily Costello, *Tara Lipinski: Triumph on Ice*, pp. 3-4.

[189] Source: Ekaterina Gordeeva, *My Sergei*, pp. 24-25.

[190] Source: Kerri Strug, *Landing on My Feet*, p. 132.

[191] Source: S.H. Burchard, *Dorothy Hamill*, p. 53.

[192] Source: Tara Lipinski, *Tara Lipinski: Triumph on Ice*, pp. 23-24.

[193] Source: Keith Elliot Greenberg, *Zack's Story*, pp. 4-5, 10.

[194] Source: Norton Mockridge, *A Funny Thing Happened ...*, p. 20.

[195] Source: William H. Sessions, collector, *More Quaker Laughter*, p. 99.

[196] Source: Doreen Gonzales, *Diego Rivera: His Art, His Life*, p. 21.

[197] Source: S.H. Burchard, *Dorothy Hamill*, p. 48.

[198] Source: Grace Fox, *Everyday Etiquette*, p. 25.

[199] Source: Joe Garagiola, *It's Anybody's Ballgame*, p. 272.

[200] Source: Bethany Kandel, *Trevor's Story*, p. 7.

[201] Source: Jeanne Marie Laskas, *We Remember*, p. 59.

[202] Source: Harvey Mindess, *The Chosen People?*, pp. 76-77.

[203] Source: JoAnn Bren Guernsey, *Tipper Gore: Voice for the Voiceless*, pp. 58-59.

[204] Source: Jay David, *The Life and Humor of Robin Williams*, p. 3.

[205] Source: Robert E. Drennan, editor, *The Algonquin Wits*, p. 148.

[206] Source: Bethany Kandel, *Trevor's Story*, p. 22.

[207] Source: Chastity Bono, *Family Outing*, pp. 212-213.

[208] Source: Logan Munger Brady, *Amusing Anecdotes*, p. 284.

[209] Source: Mary Northrup, *American Computer Pioneers*, p. 39.

[210] Source: Rusty E. Frank, *Tap!*, pp. 142-143.

[211] Source: Joe E. Brown, *Laughter is a Wonderful Thing*, p. 200.

[212] Source: Art Linkletter, *Oops!*, pp. x-xi.

[213] Source: Lewis C. Henry, *Humorous Anecdotes About Famous People*, p. 132.

[214] Source: Bernice Kanner, *The 100 Best TV Commercials*, p. 199.

[215] Source: Arthur Marx, *Life With Groucho*, p. 256.

[216] Source: James Fadiman and Robert Frager, *Essential Sufism*, p. 172.

[217] Source: Richard Watson, *The Philosopher's Diet*, p. 104.

[218] Source: Rusty E. Frank, *Tap!*, p. 139.

[219] Source: Kate Clinton, *Don't Get Me Started*, pp. 58-59.

[220] Source: William H. Sessions, collector, *Laughter in Quaker Grey*, p. 21.

[221] Source: Christine Brennan, *Inside Edge*, p. 68.

[222] Source: Yitta Halberstam Mandelbaum, *Holy Brother*, p. xiv, pp. 33-34.

[223] Source: Harvey Mindess, *The Chosen People?*, pp. 38-39.

[224] Source: Judith Pinkerton Josephson, *Nikki Giovanni: Poet of the People*, p. 49.

[225] Source: Angelica Shirley Carpenter and Jean Shirley, *Frances Hodgson Burnett: Beyond the Secret Garden*, p. 119.

[226] Source: Jay David, *The Life and Humor of Robin Williams*, p. 79.

[227] Source: Bruce Laffey, *Beatrice Lillie*, p. 88.

[228] Source: Art Linkletter, *I Didn't Do It Alone*, p. 88.

[229] Source: Marilyn Hall and Rabbi Jerome Cutler, *The Celebrity Kosher Cookbook*, p. 35.

[230] Source: Denise M. Jordan, *Walter Dean Myers: Writer for Real Teens*, p. 90.

[231] Source: Jeanne Marie Laskas, *We Remember*, p. 95.

[232] Source: Alyene Porter, *Papa was a Preacher*, pp. 106-107, 109.

[233] Source: Robert E. Pike, *Granite Laughter and Marble Tears*, p. 63.

[234] Source: Whitney Stewart, *Aung San Suu Kyi: Fearless Voice of Burma*, p. 53.

[235] Source: Constance Benson, *Mainly Players*, p. 104.

[236] Source: Michael Thomas Ford, *The Voices of AIDS*, pp. 64-65.

[237] Source: Yitta Halberstam Mandelbaum, *Holy Brother*, pp. 8-9.

[238] Source: Frank B. Gilbreth, Jr. and Ernestine Gilbreth Carey, *Cheaper by the Dozen*, p. 36.

[239] Source: Gerald Fuller, *Stories for All Seasons*, p. 65.

[240] Source: Edward K. Rowell, editor, *Humor for Preaching and Teaching*, p. 183.

[241] Source: William R. Sanford and Carl R. Green, *Dorothy Hamill*, pp. 29, 46.

[242] Source: Gene Ward and Dick Hyman, *Football Wit and Humor*, p. 5.

[243] Source: Irvin C. Poley and Ruth Verlenden Poley, *Friendly Anecdotes*, pp. 17-18.

[244] Source: Gene Ward and Dick Hyman, *Football Wit and Humor*, p. 83.

[245] Source: Sharon Salzberg, *A Heart as Wide as the World*, pp. 10-11.

[246] Source: Brandon Marie Miller, *Buffalo Gals: Women of the Old West*, p. 19.

[247] Source: Elliott Caplin, *Al Capp Remembered*, pp. 14-15.

[248] Source: Mildred and Milton Lewis, *Famous Modern Newspaper Writers*, p. 32.

[249] Source: Mary Malone, *Will Rogers: Cowboy Philosopher*, p. 81.
[250] Source: H. Allen Smith, *The Compleat Practical Joker*, p. 258.

www.ingramcontent.com/pod-product-compliance
Lightning Source LLC
Chambersburg PA
CBHW031453130726

47989CB00003B/1367